NEWS ACCOUNTS OF ATTACKS ON WOMEN:

A Comparison of Three Toronto Newspapers

Sophia E. Voumvakis
and
Richard V. Ericson

Research Report of the
Centre of Criminology
University of Toronto

1984

© Sophia E. Voumvakis

Richard V. Ericson

Centre of Criminology

University of Toronto

Toronto, 1984

ISBN 0-919584-60-8

Canadian Cataloguing in Publication Data

Voumvakis, Sophia E. (Sophia Elizabeth), 1957-
   News accounts of attacks on women

(Research report of the Centre of Criminology,
University of Toronto ; 20)
Bibliography: p.
ISBN 0-919584-60-8

1. Women in the press - Ontario - Toronto - Case
studies.   2. Violence in mass media - Ontario -
Toronto - Case studies.   I. Ericson, Richard V., 1948-
II. University of Toronto. Centre of Criminology.
III. Title.   IV. Series.

PN4914.W58V68 1984   070.4'33'088042   C84-098713-7

ACKNOWLEDGEMENTS

We are grateful to Janet Chan and Anthony Doob for comments on earlier drafts, and to Rita Donelan, Marie Pearce and Wendy Burgess for their willing and first rate work in the production of this monograph.

This report is part of a much larger research programme, "Understanding News of Deviance and Control", funded by the Centre of Criminology, University of Toronto, and the Social Sciences and Humanities Research Council (Project Grant No. 410-83-0748). This research has also been indirectly facilitated by the Contributions Program to the Centre of Criminology of the Ministry of the Solicitor General, Canada.

Sophia E. Voumvakis
Richard V. Ericson

TABLE OF CONTENTS

LIST OF TABLES

CHAPTER ONE

NEWS ORGANIZATION, ACCOUNTS OF CRIME, AND MORAL PANIC

Introduction

Accounts of crime incidents, crime control efforts, and issues in the administration of criminal justice are a dominant feature of news media content (Ditton and Duffy, 1982; Dussuyer, 1979; Graber, 1980; for a review, see Garofalo, 1981). In particular, there is a daily menu of news reports about individual incidents of crime and other forms of deviance, with over-emphasis upon sexual assault and other categories of violence (ibid.). These accounts of crime incidents have a standard news format. In any given instance the reporter simply changes the details of what was involved, who was involved, and what the authorities have done or are planning to do about it. These items have so little variation that they have the character of "eternal recurrence" (Rock, 1973). They seem to entertain, titillate, and disturb one's sense of order more than provide useful information or knowledge.

On occasion news workers (including journalists and their sources) link together a series of crime incidents to create a wider framework and theme in the news. Either on their own or after talking with sources, journalists invoke lay theories about possible patterns which are indicated by several crime incidents. They initially "test" these theories with their sources, and continue to do this until they themselves, as well as their editors and news competitors, decide that the "newsworthiness" of doing so has been exhausted. For example, several violent assaults in a city that remain unsolved might be linked by journalists on the basis of the assumption that the same suspect may be involved, and police sources are "pressed" on this interpretation. Additionally, journalists might speculate that this is indicative of a new trend and signifies a deterioration of life in the city, or at least life for a particular victimized group of citizens. Various interest groups, political authorities, crime control authorities, and experts are used as sources to display a range of opinion on the matter. They recite causes, and what should be, can be, and is being done about it. This journalistic canvassing is not done on the basis of systematic surveys which culminate in a report in the mould of social science, but on a daily basis of seeing if there is another incident to sustain the theme, or another source to provide a slightly different account, or previously used sources to update their views, positions and recommendations (Epstein, 1974).

Cohen (1972) was the first to point out that these practices of journalists - as they transact with, use, and are used by sources - yield a product that creates a sense of "moral panic" among the population who consume it. In Cohen's words,

> Societies appear to be subject, every now and then, to periods of moral panic. A condition, episode, person or group of persons emerges to become defined as a threat to societal values and interests; its nature is presented in a stylized and stereotypical fashion by the mass media; the moral barricades are manned by editors, bishops, politicans and other right-thinking people; socially accredited experts pronounce their diagnoses and solutions; ways of coping are evolved or (more often) resorted to; the condition then disappears, submerges or deteriorates and becomes more visible. Sometimes the object of the panic is quite novel and at other times it is something which has been in existence long enough, but suddenly appears in the limelight. Sometimes the panic passes over and is forgotten, expect in folklore and collective memory; at other times it has more serious and long-lasting repercussions and might produce such changes as those in legal and social policy or even in the way society conceives itself.

(ibid.: 9)

Cohen mapped out the dimensions of a moral panic as it evolved around the theme of violence and vandalism among groups of youths in Britain. Since then other researchers have examined the moral panic phenomenon on topics such as mugging in Britain (Hall et al., 1978), crimes against the elderly in New York (Fishman, 1978), and sexual assault and other forms of violence against children in Toronto (Ng, 1981). In the work of Cohen, and of Hall et al., the news accounts of threat to established order are portrayed as emanating from identifiable types of offenders with particular social characteristics. In the work of Fishman and of Ng, the news accounts of threat are seen as being directed at identifiable types of victims with particular social characteristics ("weak" and "vulnerable" senior citizens and children). In all cases these analyses suggest that certain features of news organization, as these articulate with what journalists regard as adequate accounts of crime and social problems, generate a moral panic that strikes a responsive cord among individual citizens, interest groups, legal control agents, and elected representatives. A "culture of public problems" (Gusfield, 1981) evolves which takes on a character and agenda of its own, only partially overlapping with the particular crime control problem to which it was originally addressed. The moral panic becomes the occasion for playing out in public the deep structure of values that are dominant in the culture and their implications for social control and social order.

In this report we examine aspects of a moral panic regarding attacks on women which was sustained for several months in 1982 in Toronto. We accomplish this by a systematic content analysis of news connected with this panic as reported in three Toronto newspapers. This work builds upon existing research in this area, but is designed to go beyond previous work in several respects.

We take a more systematic and quantitative approach to news content than previous researchers. This allows us to specify more precisely the range of sources who were used in sustaining the theme, the frequency of their use, and how they were used. In terms of how they were used, we are interested in particular in how they were mobilized to create images of "the locus of the problem", i.e. to what factors or social forces can the problem be attributed, and what remedial action is necessary to contain it? Our approach also allows us to address the important question of variation among news organizations: the extent to which they all pick up the thematic agenda and present similar images of the phenomenon via using similar sources who say similar things about the locus of the problem and its remedies. We also consider systematically news organization variation in the use of primary news slots (hard news stories) and secondary news slots (editorials, letters to the editor, opinion columns, features) to perpetuate the thematic agenda and the various views and images of it (cf. Hall et al., 1978). Mapping variation in terms of different news organizations, news space, sources, and their accounting for problems allows us to consider the extent to which news media are "mass media" in the sense of giving uniform coverage; or whether they are significantly different and thereby provide a varied marketplace of ideas, and ultimately knowledge, vital to a pluralistic democracy.

The Attacks on Women Moral Panic: A Preliminary Overview

During the summer months of 1982 there was a 'moral panic' in the city of Toronto in relation to attacks on women. On May 29th the three Toronto daily newspapers, the Globe and Mail, Toronto Sun, and Toronto Star, reported the rape and murder of Jennifer Isford; on June 22nd the rape and murder of Christine Prince was reported; on July 1st the newspapers reported the beating and rape of a young woman in High Park, which left her hospitalized in very serious condition; on July 19th the rape and murder of Judy Anne Deslisle was reported; and, on October 10th the murder of Kathy Alma Brosseau, "...Metro's latest sex-murder victim" (Toronto Star, Oct. 10, 1982: A1), was reported. In addition to these incidents, which received particular emphasis and play, the three Toronto area newspapers reported a number of other rapes, attempted rapes, and other types of assault against women. During the last months of the summer and into the early months of the autumn, reports about women who had mysteriously disappeared were also connected to the thematic agenda of "violence against women", the basic message of which was that the city of Toronto had experienced a surge of violence against women. Indeed, the editor of a magazine wrote, "it was as if, suddenly, somebody had declared violent, anonymous war on the women of the city where I live" (Quest, September, 1982:5).

In addition to the numerous occurrences that were reported under this theme there were reports on the reactions, actions, and demands of individual citizens, citizens' groups, elected officials, and others. Advice was proffered by the experts on the best precautionary measures to adopt and on more long-term solutions to the problem.

It has been argued that during periods of moral panic particular groups in society charged with social control functions may encourage the perception of a crime wave in order to further their own organizational interests (Fishman, 1978). In the present instance the reaction of various groups to these incidents was explicitly a political matter, with a range of citizens' groups, politicians, law enforcement agencies, and others using the perception of a wave of violence against women as a vehicle to articulate their own organizational positions, goals and interests.

For example, in September 1982, when the Rape Crisis Centre was actively engaged in its annual fund raising drive, the appeal which appeared in the Toronto Star was framed within the terms of the moral panic. The essential "pitch" was that, in light of the "fact" of a recent surge of attacks on women, the Rape Crisis Centre was needed now more than ever.

> Rape Crisis Centre needs help
>
> April 11, 1980: Barbara Schlifer, raped and stabbed to death in the hallway of her apartment building.
>
> May 28, 1982: Jenny Isford, raped and strangled on her way home from work, left dead on a neighbour's lawn.

June 22, 1982: Christine Prince, a nanny from Wales, raped and battered to death, her body found floating in a stream.

June 30, 1982: A 23-year-old woman, beaten on the head with a rock and raped in High Park.

July 12, 1982: Claudia Geburt, raped and stabbed to death in her apartment, on her 21st birthday.
Each of these is a name to shake our hearts with horror and rage.

...Unless $20,000 can be found in a hurry, the service starts to crumble this week. (Toronto Star, Sept. 17, 1982:C1).

During this period the Guardian Angels, a New York City based organization for mobilizing private individuals to conduct street patrols in their own cities, began a campaign to set up patrols in Toronto. Their campaign was based on arguing that the police were not performing their task adequately and that one of the consequences of this inefficiency was the "increase" in attacks against women. The "attacks on women" phenomenon was explicitly used as a justification of the need for the presence of the Guardian Angels in Toronto. Although the police authorities and some city officials argued that the group was not needed or wanted, and further charged that they "...had a vested interest in arousing the fears of Metro residents" (Toronto Sun, July 5, 1982:4) others were presented as being more open. For example, the Toronto Sun (July 5, 1982:4) reported that "Toronto Ald. Tony O'Donohue said he sees a place for the group here in the wake of four murders of young women and the brutal rape of another."

Reporters interviewed women in Toronto in order to capture their feelings on what had happened and on how these occurrences had affected them. One headline read, "Fear stalks Metro women after cheerleader's slaying" (Toronto Star, June 3, 1982:A3).

Various seminars and courses were set up in order to advise women how to protect themselves. Reporters interviewed the experts on crime and prevention, and they gave advice to women on how they could avoid such a fate from befalling them.

> Common sense is the best form of self defence for women, experts say in the wake of sexual assaults in Toronto. Police and martial arts experts agree that avoiding dangerous situations in the first place is the smart policy for women alone, especially at night.

(Toronto Sun, July 11, 1982:40)

Some enterprising business minds capitalized on the fear experienced by women to market various products that women could use in the course of an attack, for example the "Screamer", while others offered self defence courses.

A businessman started a petition demanding tougher bail and parole laws for violent criminals. He was quoted as saying, "I'm tired of opening the paper and reading about rapes and murders that have been committed by criminals out on parole" (Toronto Star, June 28, 1982:A7).

A group of citizens set up a vigil in High Park in July. One story read in part,

> Outraged by the rash of violent attacks against women in Metro recently, a group of concerned men and women started a 10-day vigil in High Park yesterday to call attention to the crimes (Toronto Star, July 22, 1982:A6).

A "Take Back the Night" March, an annual event held in September and sponsored by the Toronto Rape Crisis Centre, was held instead in July "...because of the recent murders and rapes in Metro" (Toronto Star, July 24, 1982:A2).

Metro Chairman Paul Godfrey "...called for an examination of bail, parole and mandatory supervision arrangements" (Globe and Mail, July 16,

1982:1-2). North York mayor Mel Lastman called upon the provincial
government to allow Metro municipalities the jurisdiction to pass laws
banning hitchiking because that "...would save a lot of lives" (Toronto
Sun, July 14, 1982:4). North York controller Esther Shiner called for
the reinstatement of a law requiring that employers provide
transportation home for their female employees leaving work between
midnight and 6 a.m..

A three hour public forum on Women and Safety was sponsored by the
YWCA. Topics included how women should deal with their fear and anger,
precautions that women should adopt in order to avoid attack, and self
defence.

In early August, a change in the Metro Police homicide squad was
announced. The Toronto Star and the Toronto Sun linked this "shake
down" with the unsolved rapes and murders that had occurred, thus
encompassing this event under the theme of "violence against women".

> Police sources say that unsolved Metro sex slayings
> of cheerleader Jenny Isford, Welsh nanny Christine
> Prince and Claudia Geburt, who was raped and stabbed
> to death in her Leslie St. home on July 12, are among
> the main reasons for changes in the homicide squad.
>
> (Toronto Star, Aug. 7, 1982:A1)

These various reports typify the range of constituencies consulted,
the imagery of the problem, and its solution, created within the three
Toronto newspapers under study. A more systematic and fine-grained
analysis is presented in Chapters Three, Four and Five. At this
juncture it is necessary to elaborate upon the nature of news production
and products as they relate to the generation of moral panics.

Journalist Ideology, News Organization, and Crime Waves

News workers are faced daily with massive amounts of material from which must be fashioned relatively few news stories. There are two major components to the ideological system by which journalists identify and interpret news. The first relates to the recipe knowledge (Berger and Luckmann, 1967) by which journalists accomplish their everyday work. Journalists employ an integrated framework of categories, concepts and relevancies grounded in their particular mode of existence (Tuchman, 1978). This provides the background assumptions with which to understand what is to be treated as an event, what is to be treated as a fact about the event, and how that fact is to be interpreted and used. It is unlikely that this working ideology is consciously produced by individuals; rather, it is an unconscious construction that structures perception and thought so that certain realities are included while others are excluded. This serves to constitute their ideology as a way of knowing that is also a way of not knowing (ibid.; Fishman, 1980).

The second component of this ideological system is what Chibnall (1977) has termed the "professional imperatives of journalism", or professional ideology. This professional ideology includes, among other elements, conceptions of fairness, impartiality, balance, and objectivity.

Fishman (1978) has argued that crime waves often do not have any basis in other measures of reality (e.g. police statistics). Rather, crime waves "...are constructs of the mass media..." (ibid.:531) and their sources. A crime wave in the news media begins with newsworkers who deploy their working and professional ideologies in establishing a theme for their selection of suitable news items. "Crime waves are little more than the continued and heavy coverage of numerous occurrences which journalists report as a single topic (for example 'crimes against the elderly')" (ibid.).

The news theme can be conceptualized as a unifying concept. It serves to present an event or a number of different events in terms of some broader concept. In the present instance the Toronto newspapers presented various incidents of attacks on women, police and other crime control actions, and public reactions, under the theme of violence against women. Perceiving themes is useful in news work itself. The selection process can be more easily managed if items can be selected and sorted according to possible themes. Indeed, Hall et al. (1978) have argued that newsworkers have, as one of their recipe rules, an increased tendency to report events that can be made part of an existing newsworthy theme. Seeing themes in news leads to the inclusion of particular material and ignoring or selective exclusion of other possibilities. This process is a component in the ideological production of crime (cf. Tuchman, 1978).

All crime themes have the potential to become crime waves. However, one news organization alone is unlikely to create a crime wave; there must be collaboration with other news organizations. This collaboration is not a conscious conspiracy but rather is a function of a daily process in newswork. All news organizations rely on other news media in order to derive their sense of "what's news today". This process allows for a continuity of news judgements, so for example a specific incident or theme appearing in a morning newspaper might be picked up by an evening newspaper, perhaps with more incidents or details. Journalists will begin to notice each other's reporting on a particular crime theme, and this will serve to reinforce their notion that this kind of crime is news (Gordon and Heath, 1981). Sacks (1972:333) has argued that journalists have established a consistency rule: "...every crime incident that can be seen as an instance of the theme, will be seen and reported as such."

Fishman (1978) refers to this as a "crime wave dynamic". However, he argues that an additional element is required before a crime theme grows into a crime wave: "there must be a continuous supply of crime incidents that can be seen as instances of a theme" (ibid.:530) (emphasis in original). It is in this regard that sources become important.

Journalists and their Sources

Journalists operate within their occupational culture, social organizational constraints of the news organization which employs them, and the constraints constituted by source organizations.

Reporters will tend to position themselves so that they can have regular and routine access to the institutions that produce useful news items on a fairly consistent basis. This situation arises in part from the organizational constraints of news production. Reporters are expected to produce a certain amount of news copy on a regular basis while under various organizational constraints, for example time restrictions and scarcity of resources (Gordon and Heath, 1981). One solution in coping with these constraints is to place oneself in a position to acquire, at regular intervals, useful information about events that can be transformed into news.

A second reason why journalists go to particular institutions for information relates to the professional ideology which structures their work. The "objectivity paradigm" provides a distinction between fact and opinion: news reports are deemed to be factual when they are grounded in the authoritative statements of experts in the particular fields covered by the news story. Journalists will thus turn to the accredited representatives, the "authorized knowers", from the major institutions to structure their stories, and obtain accounts from a range of such legitimate positions to convey objectivity.

In the case of crime news the police are the ideal institution by which journalists can deal with both the organizational constraints they experience and the constraints of the occupational culture. The basic facts concerning many crime events can be easily acquired from the police Major Occurrences Report. In addition police stations are generally in operation twenty-four hours a day, they are conveniently located, and sometimes have press rooms, at least at Headquarters. Moreover, the police are the accredited representatives when it comes to crime by virtue of their state assigned institutional power and position, and their 'expertise' in crime prevention gained by their daily involvement in the "fight against crime".

The police are the major source of information concerning crime available to newspapers (Fishman, 1980; Chibnall, 1977; Hall et al., 1978). Indeed, in instances of crime waves, Fishman (1978) has argued that the police have the power to either veto the crime wave by not supplying enough incidents to the media or to strengthen it by supplying appropriate instances. There are suggestions that the police may encourage the perception of particular crime waves when certain organizational benefits are to be gained, for example, an increase in resources (ibid.).

However, the power of the police to either veto or strengthen the reporting of a crime wave probably depends upon the type of crime that is the subject of the wave. It would be very difficult for the police to submerge a string of murders because of the other organizations that would be involved, especially hospitals and medical authorities. If the media were to find out about a number of incidents from sources in other organizations, this could be used to cast negative commentary upon the police.

Furthermore, the police may supply the media with statistics showing little evidence of any increase in a particular type of crime, but the media may choose to ignore them (ibid.). In relation to the attacks on women moral panic under study, the researcher was in attendance at a public forum sponsored by the YWCA where two of the speakers, a police constable and a psychologist, presented the audience with statistics showing that there had not been any increase in attacks on women during 1982 as compared with a similar time span in 1981. The following day the newspaper accounts of the discussions did not report this evidence. They did not even include the argument by the police officer and the psychologist, followed by reasons for disclaiming it based on other evidence. That is, it might have been argued that such statistics are of little value because they do not include a sufficiently long period to indicate a trend; however the news media do regularly use comparisons from one year to the next to show changes in crime. Moreover, it is possible that proportionately more of the incidents in 1981 may have occurred in different settings, for example within the family setting, whereas most incidents of 1982 took place in street settings and public places and that element was one of the primary considerations in the moral panic. Nevertheless, such questioning was not evident in any published news accounts. The fact remains that the police did attempt to discourage the perception of the moral panic by providing at least some evidence, but the newspapers decided to ignore the claim on this occasion.

Moral Panics and Uniformity of Coverage

While the police are a major source of information, especially regarding details of crime incidents for primary reports, other sources are used to express fear and loathing, explanations, and remedies, especially in "secondary" reports (Hall et al., 1978). The selection of such sources is governed by the "objectivity paradigm" as well as by the particular theme that the news media are using. Epstein (1974:271-2) has argued that the decision on who to consult as a source is partly based on thematic criteria rather than on modal criteria.

As stated previously, journalists routinely review the contents of other news organizations as part of the process by which they inform themselves of what is newsworthy. This is one aspect of "pack journalism". In some areas of news coverage, the result of this approach, combined with the process of source selection, is a uniformity in coverage across news media organizations. Studies of moral panics (Cohen, 1972; Fishman, 1978; Hall et al., 1978; Ng, 1981) lead one to assume that "pack journalism" is particularly salient at these times. Combined with the thematic agenda influence on source selection this process results in fairly uniform coverage.

These aspects of uniformity in coverage are one reason why recent research and theorizing on the media has tended to collapse all media organizations into a powerful institution that has uniform practices, products and interests. However, given that different media organizations may have different organizational and technical frameworks, and may be addressing different audience segments, it is possible that this implied uniformity in coverage is overstated. It is necessary therefore that differentiation in crime news content be studied across news organizations (Garofalo, 1981:340), a primary focus of the present research. As stated in the Introduction, previous research studies have failed to examine systematically the degree of uniformity in coverage across news organizations during periods of moral panic. This uniformity has been assumed, not demonstrated. A demonstration of relative diversity, if it exists, can lead us to question the extent to which all media organizations can be conceptualized as part of a single powerful institution.

CHAPTER TWO

RESEARCH STRATEGY

Introduction

We decided to examine the three major daily newspapers in Toronto as they gave coverage to the attacks on women theme between May 1 and October 31, 1982. As detailed below, all items were selected which included at least one attribution concerning the locus of the problem of attacks on women. This yielded a newspaper item sample of 391. The sources quoted in these items were identified, with a total of 552 sources in the 391 newspaper items. The attributions sources made, or that were inferred from their statements, concerning the locus of the problem, were also recorded, yielding a total of 605 attributions in the 391 newspaper items. Along with the type of news category (primary or secondary) in which these items were presented, the newspaper, source, and attribution concerning the locus of the problem were the variables selected for quantitative analysis.

In addition, the newspaper items over this period were scrutinized for particular features that could only be portrayed qualitatively. The layout of items and the structuring of the texts were considered in terms of what they revealed about journalistic techniques for sustaining the attacks on women theme and its attendant images.

The Newspapers Studied

At the time of the study the <u>Globe and Mail</u> published Monday to Saturday, the Toronto <u>Sun</u> Sunday to Friday and the Toronto <u>Star</u> seven days a week.

The Royal Commission on Newspapers (R.C.N.) (1981) identifies the <u>Globe and Mail</u> as a national newspaper. One distinguishing feature is in the role it plays in agenda setting for the news media in general, generating much of the news coverage and commentary on public affairs in Canada (R.C.N., 1981b:9). The Globe and Mail is considered to be at the 'quality' end of a continuum which includes 'popular' at the opposite end. It has a large 'newshole' (the proportion of reading material to advertising): approximately 45% on a typical weekday as compared to the other two Toronto newspapers which have approximately 30% each (R.C.N., 1981:76). It also has a high ratio of secondary interpretation and background to primary spot news, and a diversity of political columnists. The Globe and Mail caters to an 'elite' audience of readers, those who are interested in business and economic issues, national politics, and international affairs (R.C.N., 1981a:71).

The Toronto Sun occupies the opposite end of the continuum, being a 'popular' newspaper. The Toronto Sun is directed toward readers who want a brief look at news that is written in a lively style, strongly opinionated columns and editorials, good sports coverage, "...and generous dollops of what has given the tabloids in London's Fleet Street the generic name of 'tit-and-bum' newspapers" (ibid.:70).

The Toronto Star has the largest circulation of any newspaper in the country. The Royal Commission on Newspapers included the Toronto Star in their list of Canada's national media. However, its focus is considered to be more regional and metropolitan than the Globe and Mail, and its national influence rests more with the fact that its materials are widely syndicated (R.C.N., 1981b and 1981c). In terms of content and style this newspaper falls somewhere in between the continuum of 'quality' and 'popular' and can be classified as a 'traditional' newspaper (R.C.N., 1981c). The Toronto Star is an example of the mass circulation newspaper which seeks to appeal to readers across the board. Ottawa columnist Richard Gwyn describes this paper as operating "...on the smorgasboard technique; every reader will find something" (R.C.N., 1981a:71).

The Royal Commission on Newspapers characterizes the competition among the three newspapers in the city of Toronto as a 'coexistence' model; although in competition which each other, the newspapers compete with the understanding that they will continue to offer readers a choice. The newspapers will vie for only a portion of the market (R.C.N., 1981c:75), although obviously there is some overlap in their markets. One would expect that as a consequence of this competition structure and efforts to appeal to different audience segments, the three newspapers might show considerable diversity in coverage of a moral panic theme. The concentration of 'primary' to 'secondary' news (Hall et al., 1978:88), the choice of sources, and the identifications that these sources either explicitly or implicitly make to the locus of the problem, might vary substantially. On the other hand, the fact that news media organizations refer to each other as a guide on what to cover, the finding by other researchers that this practice is highly prevalent at times of moral panic, and the fact that sources are chosen according to the constraints imposed by the working and professional ideologies of newswork, may militate against such diversity.

News Contexts

As mentioned in Chapter One, importance has been attached by previous researchers to the distinction between primary and secondary news (Hall et al., 1978). Primary news items generally contain reports on crime incidents while secondary news items are the answers to the questions implicitly set up in the primary reports. "The formal shifts - from news to editorials, or from news to features - both depend on elaborating themes already present in first - order news presentation" (ibid.).

It might be predicted that a newspaper such as the Globe and Mail, which is classified as having a higher ratio of interpretation and background to spot news, would have a greater tendency to do proportionately more secondary reporting than a popular newspaper such

as the Toronto <u>Sun</u>. It was felt that a systematic analysis of the area
in the newspaper where items concerning attacks on women were found
might point to some diversity in coverage among the three newspapers
during the moral panic. Seven different categories of this variable
were formulated.

<u>News stories of incidents</u> included crime incidents, follow-ups on
particular incidents, reports on the state of police investigations, and
reports on the actions and demands of various organizations, be they
citizen or official, in response to a particular occurrence or
occurrences.

<u>News stories of court cases</u> included reports on bail hearings,
reports on the progress of trials, and reports dealing with the
sentencing of convicted offenders. Both news stories and news stories
of court cases are within Hall <u>et al.</u>'s (1978) definition of primary
reports.

<u>News features</u> included major articles that contained material on the
reactions of various groups or individuals, e.g. "polls" conducted on
the streets of Toronto asking women about their fears; and, articles
dealing with a particular aspect of the phenomenon, such as what
motivates some men to rape and the treatment of sex offenders within the
correctional system.

<u>Opinion columns</u> are those in which an identified individual
journalist regularly addresses her or his opinion on some incident or
isssue.

<u>Editorials</u> are similar to opinion columns, except it is the
newspaper editor and her or his editorial staff who express their
opinion. In the newspapers studied it was a practice not to identify
the author of the editorial. Both opinion columns and editorials invoke
the claim of speaking on behalf of the public (<u>ibid.</u>). Features,

opinion columns, and editorials are all secondary reports.

The letters to the editor space provides for citizen input. Letters to the editor have not been subject to much previous research. The selection of letters to print is in the hands of the editor, and different newspapers are known to have a different flavour to their letters section. Hall and associates (ibid.) found that most of the letters which they studied during a "mugging" panic took off from a point the primary news reports had been stressing as newsworthy. These authors further argue that one of the major functions of this type of column is to stimulate controversy, provoke public response, and encourage debate. It also presents the image that the pages of the newspaper are open to views that the newspaper itself may not necessarily adhere to, although it remains an empirical question whether this is the case.

The citizen's opinion column serves basically the same function as the letters column, only in this type of column the citizen is answering a question posed either by the newspaper, (e.g. they may telephone in an answer as in the Toronto Star's "What Do You Think?" column), or by the reporter interviewing them in the street (e.g. The Toronto Sun's "You Said it" column). The Globe and Mail did not have a citizen's opinion column.

Sources

As stated in Chapter One, the research literature reveals that working and professional ideologies of journalists, as they articulate with the theme being pursued, structure source selection and can lead to uniformity in coverage. However, it may be that the three newspaper organizations studied are not all under the same organizational constraints; they may have a different sense of newsworthiness, in the context of catering to different readerships. These factors may allow for some diversity in the selection of sources. For example, a newspaper which is seen to be catering to a professional and business readership, such as the Globe and Mail, may be more inclined to refer to sources with various socially recognized credentials to inform their discussions.

Although other researchers (Chibnall, 1977; Fishman, 1978, 1980) have shown that the police and the courts are the primary source of information concerning crime news, researchers have tended not to record systematically the sources used by the newspapers. It was felt that a systematic recording of the sources used by the newspapers to inform their coverage of attacks on women would add some important knowledge.

In the course of the newspaper search that was undertaken, five source categories were formulated. These include criminal justice system sources, individual citizens, experts and organizational representatives, journalists, and the participants.

The criminal justice system category includes the police, judges, defence lawyers, crown attorneys, and matters brought out during the course of a trial that could not be directly attributed to anyone in particular.

The individual citizens category includes citizens interviewed by reporters who were not associated with any particular organization; citizens who wrote into the newspaper and whose letters appeared in the letters to the editor column (there was only one letter whose author was identified as a member of an organized group); relatives, friends, and neighbours of the victim; and local celebrities (television personalities, models, etc.).

The category labelled experts and organizational representatives includes a wide range of sources. Expert types include psychiatrist, medical doctor, social scientist, professor, author, and martial arts specialist. Spokespersons represented a variety of organizations, including various religious organizations, a professional football team's cheerleading organization (one victim during the period researched was a member of this organization), an elected political representative, the Toronto Transit Commission, the Vancouver Sun newspaper, a Lady Fitness Centre, Henry Farm Community Interest Association, Citizens United for Safety and Justice, Guardian Angels, Pink Ribbon Committee (a coalition of a number of women's organizations), Toronto Rape Crisis Centre, Task Force on Women and Violence, League for Human Rights B'nai B'rith, Manitoba Action Committee for the Status of Women, Parkdale Action Committee against Racism, Women's Coalition Against Sexist Advertising, National Committee on the Status of Women, Canadian Jewish Congress, Ontario Status of Women Council, Judy LaMarsh Centre for Research on Violence, and a Nanny Agency (one victim during the period researched was a Nanny).

The fourth category, journalists, includes the writers of editorials and opinion columns. Journalists were also counted as sources in news stories, news stories of court cases, and news features, if they gave accounts suggesting the locus of the problem without attribution to an outside source.

The fifth category, the participants, includes the victim and the offender. The small numbers in this category entailed not including it in most of the tabular analyses which follow.

Locus of the Problem

Some analysts of the media argue that media organizations operate using the "consensual paradigm" of the dominant culture in order to make sense of the events in the world (Young, 1981). Underlying the media's presentation of reality is a belief in the essential justice and desirability of the present organization of society. A high degree of consensus is presumed to exist about what is valuable and desirable, and about how social life should be regulated and controlled. Deviance, which Erikson (1966) argues makes up the majority of what we call news, presents a threat to this image of consensus. However, news accounts ultimately serve to neutralize the threat and reproduce images of order. For example, acts are depicted by the news media as sub-human "...as not involving the power of free choice which the vast majority of citizens are seen to possess" (Young, 1981:232), as a means of neutralizing the threat. Moreover, events that are presented in the media "...are to be understood not by reference to certain structural arrangements and social processes but either (a) as the work of individuals or (b) through their effects on individuals" (Chibnall, 1977:27).

Given the argument that events will be presented within a restricted world view and understood either as the work of individuals, or through their effects on individuals, it is necessary to investigate the range of accounts of the problem that are given. Of course, this must be related to who gives the accounts, and whether the dominant cultural view is portrayed in a similar manner in all newspapers.

Images of problems presented during moral panics have implications for the legitimacy of social control processes and practices in society. As Smart and Smart (1978) report from their study of the portrayal of rape in newspapers, when accounts of motivation for rape were presented they tended to perpetuate the commonly held belief that rape is simply the outcome of sexual frustration or arousal. They further found that in many instances the news report contained a warning or a caution to women, such as where and where not to walk, what time not to go out, how not to behave, and what not to wear. They concluded that, "the cumulative effect of press reports of rape is to remind women of their vulnerability, to create an atmosphere of fear and to suggest, as a solution, that women should withdraw to the traditional shelter of the domestic sphere and the protection of _their_ men" (_ibid._:102) (emphasis in the original). Given the fact that for the vast majority of citizens the major source of information concerning crime is the mass media - for example, Graber (1980:49-50) reports that 95% of the respondents she interviewed "designated the mass media as their primary source of information about crime and criminal justice" - this type of representation of attacks on women in newspapers has obvious implications for the social control of women. An examination of attributions to the locus of the problem made by sources allows consideration of implications for the social control of women that some of these attributions may contain.

Based on the newspaper search, five categories were created regarding the locus of the problem: attributing the problem to the victim, to the offender, to the criminal justice system and/or policing, to the portrayal of women, or to some type of social pathology.

Examples of the type of statements that were deemed to be locating the problem in relation to the victim included references to the victim taking a shortcut through a ravine late at night, hitchiking, accepting a ride home from a stranger, dressing provocatively, leaving her door unlocked, drinking alone in a bar, sunbathing in a secluded area by herself, and taking a man home from a bar. In addition, recommendations from police, experts and citizen sources that such circumstances should be avoided (as a crime prevention precaution) were also included in this category.

Statements that were classified as attributing the locus of the problem to a factor in the offender included describing offenders as 'sexually immature', as a 'sexual sadist', as a 'weirdo', as a 'sick individual', as a 'lunatic' and as a 'pervert'. This category also included remarks about offenders' 'anti-social personality disorder', 'serious mental problems', 'mental illness', and 'inability to handle rejection'. Offenders were further described as 'drug addict', 'alcholic', as having a 'terrible sex urge', and as having 'poor impulse control'. Other sources made references to the offenders' upbringing. For example, some offenders were said to come from violent families and subjected to abuse as children, some were described as products of sexually repressive families, and some the products of broken homes.

Statements from which it could be deemed that sources were attributing the locus of the problem to <u>policing</u> tended to mention with regularity that the police department lacked the ability to deter potential sex offenders. Attributions to the <u>criminal justice system</u> included references to the failure of legislators to enact or to support legislation to deal with sexual offenders; bail laws; the judicial system's leniency in sentencing sex offenders; the lack of treatment received by sex offenders once they entered the correctional system; the mandatory supervision program; and the parole system.

Statements that were categorized as locating the source of the problem to the <u>portrayal of women</u> involved some discussion of pornography and its possible relationship to violence against women, and to the portrayal of women in the media in general.

Attributions to some type of <u>social pathology</u> included structurally located defects in gender relations, the malaise of the economy, public apathy, and racism (all related to one incident with an anti-semitic element).

There are several important points to bear in mind regarding these categorizations.

We have counted as a "locus of the problem" the inclusion of certain primary facts about incidents of attacks on women. As discussed in subsequent chapters, journalists repeatedly cited the facts surrounding incidents of attacks on women during the course of follow-up stories, features, opinion column statements, etc. In particular, they repeatedly mentioned circumstances surrounding the incident, such as "the victim was out alone at 1:00 a.m.", "the victim took a shortcut through a secluded area," etc. We argue that as these "facts" were consistently reiterated by journalists at almost every available opportunity, they were elevated to the position of having almost "causal" connection and thus conveyed an image of the victim as the locus of the problem. Heath, Gordon and LeBailly (1980) argue that information concerning the general climate or situation surrounding the crime are more likely to be provided in news stories about rape than in news stories of other crimes. One reasonable inference is that the inclusion of such information contributes to the imagery of locating the problem with the victim.

Another point to bear in mind is that what we identify as "locus of the problem" also can be construed as, and/or has implications for, "what should be done" about the problem. For example, "blaming the victim" in terms of dress, being out alone in potentially dangerous places, and other habits, can also be "read" as recommendations concerning how to prevent being attacked. An analogy can be made with news accounts of break and enter offences in which it is repeatedly reported that doors or windows were unlocked, locks were inadequate and that there were other security deficiences. The implied recommendation is that citizens should take steps to make their premises more secure, and the possible effect is that there will be a greater security consciousness, increased security practices, and an attendant restriction on lifestyle.

These points illustrate that there is considerable subjectivity involved in "reading" news accounts regarding the locus of the problem. The coding was undertaken by Voumvakis and there were no systematic checks for reliability.

To summarize, this research systematically records the coverage of three newspapers during a moral panic surrounding attacks on women. Three major variables were selected for quantitative comparisons among the three newspapers: the area in the newspapers where the item appeared, the sources used, and the attributions to the locus of the problem that were made. It was decided further to examine the implications that some of these attributions had for dominant ideology regarding social control of women, and to highlight this through the use of qualitative analysis of particular news items.

CHAPTER THREE

CONTEXTS AND SOURCES OF NEWS OF ATTACKS ON WOMEN

Introduction

Over the six month period under study, all three newspapers persisted in sustaining the attacks on women theme, but to varying degrees. The Globe and Mail had 50 items, the Toronto Sun 177 items, and the Toronto Star 164 items related to the theme and which included attributions as to the locus of the problem. We do not know precisely the total news space available in each newspaper over this period, which would allow us to state the relative proportion of coverage given in each newspaper to the theme. However, it is reasonable to conclude that the Toronto Sun and Toronto Sun gave very extensive coverage of the theme. On the other hand the Globe and Mail gave it considerably less attention.

News Contexts

As detailed in Table 3:1, there are few substantial differences among the three newspapers in terms of the news contexts in which attacks on women stories were reported. Approximately two-thirds of all items on the theme appeared in primary news story contexts, with little variation among the three newspapers. Since the Globe and Mail is regarded as having a higher ratio of secondary interpretation and background to primary spot news (R.C.N., 1981), especially in comparison to a popular newspaper such as the Toronto Sun, it would have been reasonable to predict that it would have had a relatively greater proportion of secondary news, especially features, on the theme. However this turned out not to be the case. Perhaps the theme remained too local in character for the Globe and Mail, as a more national newspaper, to give it more extensive attention for secondary reporting.

TABLE 3:1

NEWS CONTEXTS

Newspaper

News Contexts

		Globe and Mail %	Toronto Sun %	Toronto Star %	Totals %	N
Primary	News Story	66.0	57.1	51.8	56.0	219
	News Story of Court Case	10.0	10.7	13.4	11.7	46
	News Feature	6.0	2.3	5.5	4.1	16
	Opinion Column	4.0	6.2	2.4	4.3	17
Secondary	Editorials	2.0	1.1	4.3	2.6	10
	Letters to the Editor	12.0	17.5	22.0	18.7	73
	Citizen Opinion Columns	0.0	5.1	0.6	2.6	10
	Col. %	100.0	100.0	100.0	100.0	
	Total N	50	177	164		391
	Row %	12.7	45.4	41.9	100.0	

df = 4   p< .10 x^2 = 9.49

This x^2 calculation is based on three categories:
(1) news story, news story of court case; (2) news feature, opinion column, editorials; (3) letters to editor, citizen opinion columns.

There was some difference among the three newspapers in the use of letters to the editor and citizen opinion columns for giving play to the attacks on women theme. The Toronto Sun and Toronto Star made proportionately greater use of the letters to the editor column than did the Globe and Mail. In terms of absolute numbers, the Toronto Sun had 31 letters on the theme, the Toronto Star had 36, while the Globe and Mail had only 6. Furthermore, the Globe and Mail had no citizen opinion columns similar to the ones available in the Toronto Sun and Toronto Star. The Toronto Sun used this type of column nine times, and the Toronto Star once, to convey the opinions of citizens about the attacks on women problem.

One explanation for these differences is the different audience segments these newspapers are directed toward. The Globe and Mail is directed more to a readership interested in business, economic issues, national politics and the international scene, and their readers may have a greater tendency to write letters on these issues rather than on a theme such as a local moral panic about attacks on women. Hall and associates (1978) observe that the letters columns in different newspapers have different "flavours". Particular newspapers are known to select certain types of letters, and those wishing to write letters on a particular theme or issue may be more inclined to write them to a newspaper which appears to be taking a lead in furthering that theme or issue. In turn, editors can be expected to give their selective attention to letters which "fit" with the themes they decide to promote and sustain.

Another aspect of these differences is that the Toronto Star, and especially the Toronto Sun, pursue a popular appeal which includes considerable individual citizen input in various forms. The "person on the street" is to be given her or his voice along with "the person in official office". Letters to the editor and citizen opinion columns further this, but so do the use of individual, "unofficial" citizens as sources in other news contexts. As we shall proceed to document, the

Toronto <u>Sun</u> and Toronto <u>Star</u> underscore the "vox pop" orientation by using citizen input in other news contexts much more than the <u>Globe and Mail</u>.

Sources

As cited in Chapter One, the research literature informs us about a range of social and cultural organizational elements which structure the work of journalists, including whom they consult as sources. A major theme in the research literature is that these organizational elements constrain journalists to take up the interpretations and explanations of situations and events that are produced by sources who are the representatives of legitimate institutions, and to exclude the definitions provided by those who lack formal qualifications. This structured access results in the media systematically over-emphasizing and underpinning the interpretations of the accredited spokespersons of the state and its attendant organizations and institutions, and of certified experts who are looked upon to comment with an aura of impartiality (Chibnall, 1977; Hall <u>et al</u>., 1978; Tuchman, 1978; Taylor, 1980). As their journalistically interpreted thoughts are displayed daily in the news media, these "authorized knowers" serve to reproduce symbolically society's "hierarchy of credibility".

> In any system of ranked groups, participants take it as given that members of the highest group have a right to define the way things really are...[and that] those at the top have access to a more complete picture of what is going on than anybody else. Members of lower groups will have incomplete informationn and their view of reality will be partial and distorted in consequence (Becker, 1967: 39).

The literature indicates that persons who lack organizational positions of authority or other signs of formal qualification will not be called upon as sources with frequency or regularity. Thus, one would expect that individual citizens would not be used very often as sources and that when they are used it would be in an "appropriate" news context, especially the letters to the editor or citizen opinion columns. However, turning our attention to Table 3:2, (see also Table 3:4, which we shall address later), we learn that the Toronto Star and the Toronto Sun both used individual citizens proportionately more than any other source group regarding the attacks on women theme. In the Toronto Sun, 106 out of 244 sources used, or 43%, were individual citizens without official organizational standing as an authorized knower. In the Toronto Star, 84 out of 238 sources used, or 35%, were individual citizens.

TABLE 3:2

NEWS SOURCES

Newspaper

Sources

	Globe and Mail %	Toronto Sun %	Toronto Star %	Totals %	N
Police and Criminal Justice System	28.5	19.4	23.5	22.3	123
Individual Citizens	12.9	43.4	35.3	36.1	199
Experts and Organizational Representatives	37.1	18.0	16.4	19.7	109
Journalists	12.9	14.7	22.7	17.9	99
Participants	8.6	4.5	2.1	4.0	22
Col %	100.0	100.0	100.0	100.0	
N	70	244	238		552
Row %	12.7	44.2	43.1	100.0	

df = 8   p < .01 x^2 = 40.9

Table 3:2 indicates that only the Globe and Mail gave relatively little attention to the individual citizen: only 9 out of 70 sources used, or 13%, were individual citizens. In terms of proportionate use of sources, the Globe and Mail appears to have conformed to "the hierarchy of credibility" to a much greater extent than the other two newspapers. The Globe and Mail was most likely to cite experts and organizational representatives: 37% (26/70) of the sources they cited regarding the attacks on women theme were experts or organizational representatives, compared to only 18% (44/244) in the Toronto Sun and 16% (39/238) in the Toronto Star. Moreover, in scrutinizing the source types we included in this category, we find that the Globe and Mail relied in particular on state and other official organization representatives, and experts such as psychiatrists, psychologists, and academics, while the Toronto Star and Toronto Sun made proportionately greater use of representives from citizen interest organizations and coalitions (see the listing in Chapter Two). Thus, even in this category the Toronto Star and Toronto Sun included citizens representing popular causes, while the Globe and Mail gravitated toward authorized knowers from officialdom or who were professional experts.

Table 3:2 also indicates that in terms of total coverage, the Toronto Star and Toronto Sun actually gave more citations of experts and organizational representatives than did the Globe and Mail, in addition to their overall greater use of other source types. This is a reflection of the fact that the Globe and Mail had relatively few news items and relatively few sources cited regarding the attacks on women problem.

Another way of examining these data is to include "police and criminal justice system" sources as authorized knowers from accredited organizations. If we add this category to the "experts and organizational representatives" category, we find that 46/70 (66%) of all sources cited in the Globe and Mail were authorized knowers so classified, compared to 91/244 (37%) in the Toronto Sun and 95/238 (40%)

in the Toronto _Star_. Again, proportionately the _Globe_ _and_ _Mail_ had a much greater tendency to rely on authorized knowers from officialdom or with particular professional expertise.

One explanation for this finding relates to the different types of newspapers under consideration and the different audience segments they have established as readerships. The _Globe_ _and_ _Mail_, being closer to the "quality" end of the continuum and catering to a more business and professional audience, gave relative emphasis to the professional views of socially accredited experts and to other persons with institutional authority. The Toronto _Sun_, a "popular" newspaper which caters to those who prefer a brief look at the news written in a lively style, offered as a significant part of its popular view the statements of individual citizens. As we shall consider shortly, these were both persons connected in some way to the events used in sustaining the theme (e.g. relatives, friends, or neighbors of victimized women), as well as "the person in the street". Presumably their voice was deemed to have a closer affinity with the readership than the theorizing of the experts. The Toronto _Star_, as a "mass market" newspaper with a more regional focus than the _Globe_ _and_ _Mail_, used individual citizens as well as a substantial range of other source types in a manner similar to the Toronto _Sun_. With extensive and sustained coverage to the attacks on women theme, both the Toronto _Star_ and the Toronto _Sun_ employed a range of "knowers", including a substantial proportion of individual citizens, while the _Globe_ _and_ _Mail_ relied mainly on authorized knowers with scant inclusion of individual citizens.

Source Types and News Contexts

There was differential use of sources in the various news contexts among the three newspapers.

Several researchers (e.g. Chibnall, 1977, Hall _et_ _al._, 1978, Fishman, 1978) have focused on police and court spokespersons as _the_ important authorized knowers regarding crime news. It is therefore noteworthy that in terms of all sources cited in all three newspapers regarding the attacks on women problem, police and other criminal justice spokespersons accounted for only 22%. Moreover, as documented in Table 3:3, and in support of existing research findings, police and court sources were mainly used in primary news contexts. Among the three newspapers combined, 95% of police and criminal justice source citations were in primary news contexts. There was very little variation among the newspapers in this practice. These sources provided the primary facts about incidents, about developments in investigations, and about outcomes, including those cases which reached court.

TABLE 3:3

POLICE AND CRIMINAL JUSTICE SYSTEM SOURCES AND NEWS CONTEXTS

Police and Criminal Justice System Sources

News Contexts

		Newspapers				
		Globe and Mail %	Toronto Sun %	Toronto Star %	Totals %	N
Primary	News Story	70.0	74.5	67.9	70.7	87
	News Story of Court Case	15.0	23.4	28.6	24.4	30
Secondary	News Feature	15.0	2.1	3.5	4.9	6
	Col %	100.0	100.0	100.0	100.0	
	Total N	20	47	56		123
	Row %	16.3	38.2	45.5	100.0	

In the context of recounting primary facts, these sources were sometimes also used to offer an analysis or attribution of the locus of the problem. However, this was kept largely within the context of primary news items, rather than in the secondary news categories, which are more explicitly reserved for analysis and explanation. Only 6 out of 123 police and criminal justice system sources were cited in secondary news items, and then only in news features. However, it should be observed in this context that some information from police and criminal justice system sources was regularly reiterated in secondary items by journalists without citing the original sources of information. We return to this consideration at a later point.

As enumerated in Table 3:4, individual citizens were cited as sources in a range of news contexts, but in particular in the context of primary news stories and letters to the editor columns. As already stressed, the Globe and Mail rarely cited individual citizens; among the 9 citations, 6 were letters to the editor and 3 were in primary news stories. The Toronto Sun cited individual citizens extensively in primary news stories, the letter to the editor column, and its daily citizen opinion column. The Toronto Star has a similar pattern, except it cited citizens in news features to a much greater extent (16 citiations) than the Toronto Sun (4 citations) and the Globe and Mail (no citations).

There was extensive use of individual citizens in primary news contexts (85/199 or 43% of all individual citizen citations). As argued earlier, this appears to be part of the populist emphasis of the Toronto Sun, and the mass market popular emphasis of the Toronto Star. As elaborated upon in Chapters Four and Five, individual citizens in primary news contexts were cited as expressing "fear and loathing" over the events, thus functioning to support the public culture image of, and sense of, a moral panic. In particular, individual women citizens were used to "personalize" (Chibnall, 1977) the public culture problem by giving accounts of how "knowledge" of the events had affected their

TABLE 3:4

INDIVIDUAL CITIZENS AND NEWS CONTEXTS

Individual Citizens

News Contexts

Newspaper

		Globe and Mail %	Toronto Sun %	Toronto Star %	Totals %	N
Primary	News Story	33.3	47.2	34.5	42.7	85
	News Story of Court Case	0.0	0.0	0.0	0.0	0
	News Feature	0.0	3.8	19.0	10.0	20
	Opinion Column	0.0	0.9	0.0	0.5	1
Secondary	Editorials	0.0	0.0	0.0	0.0	0
	Letters to the Editor	66.7	29.2	41.7	34.7	69
	Citizens Opinion Column	0.0	18.9	4.8	12.1	24
	Col %	100.0	100.0	100.0	100.0	
	Total N	9	106	84		199
	Row %	4.5	53.3	42.2	100.0	

lives, made them fearful, and led them to take extra safety precautions. Individual citizens cited in news features were used in a similar manner (see Chapter Four for an example). This is a well documented journalistic technique. It personalizes, and thereby simplifies, as a means of engaging the reader (Chibnall, 1977). It also allows journalists to perform the "strategic ritual" of objectivity (Tuchman,

1978). That is, it protects journalists from appearing involved and
from appearing to be presenting their own version of events, even though
the interpretive practices of who is interviewed, what is asked, and
what is cited are squarely within the terms of the journalists' own fear
and loathing "frame" (cf. Goffman, 1974).

TABLE 3:5

EXPERTS AND ORGANIZATIONAL REPRESENTATIVES AND NEWS CONTEXTS

Experts and Organizational Representatives

News Contexts

Newspapers

		Globe and Mail %	Toronto Sun %	Toronto Star %	Totals %	N
Primary	News Story	69.2	79.5	53.8	67.9	74
	News Story of Court Case	0.0	18.2	12.8	11.9	13
	News Feature	15.4	0.0	28.2	13.8	15
	Opinion Column	15.4	2.3	0.0	4.6	5
Secondary	Editorials	0.0	0.0	2.6	0.9	1
	Letters to the Editor	0.0	0.0	2.6	0.9	1
	Citizen's Opinion Column	0.0	0.0	0.0	0.0	0
	Col %	100.0	100.0	100.0	100.0	
	Total N	26	44	39		109
	Row %	23.9	40.4	35.7	100.0	

Similar to patterns in citing authorized knowers from the police
and criminal justice system, experts and organizational representatives
tended to be cited in primary news contexts by all three newspapers
(Table 3:5). The major point of difference among newspapers is that the
Toronto Sun almost invariably weaved the accounts of experts and
organizational representatives into primary news contexts, while the
Globe and Mail and particularly the Toronto Star also cited these
sources in various secondary news contexts, especially in feature
articles. The data in Table 3:5 suggest a tendency of all three
newspapers, but especially the Toronto Sun, to insert expert and
organizational "knowers" accounts as a vital part of primary reporting.
Attributions about the locus of the problem of attacks on women
permeated the "hard" news columns, an inference that is supported by
qualitative scrutiny of news items as provided in subsequent chapters.
What are formally laid out as primary or hard news columns have
considerable material that is usually associated with secondary news
columns.

As mentioned in Chapter Two, we decided to treat journalists as
sources if they themselves conveyed information and attributions
regarding the locus of the problem in their own news items. As
enumerated in Table 3:6, journalists were counted as sources in this
respect in 99 instances. Given the "objectivity paradigm" it might have
been expected that journalists would have restricted their views
regarding the locus of the problem to their designated secondary slots,
namely editorial and opinion columns. However, Table 3:6 instructs us
that journalists themselves in all three newspapers gave information
relevant to attributing a locus of the problem of attacks on women in
primary news contexts. Indeed, this was the predominant context,
accounting for two-thirds of the instances overall. The Toronto Sun was
least likely to contain journalists' accounts in primary news contexts,
and most likely to use its staff opinion columnists (of which it has
many) for the purpose of conveying attributions of the lcus of the
problem. Nevertheless, the majority of journalists' attributions

TABLE 3:6

JOURNALISTS AND NEWS CONTEXTS

Journalists

News Context

Newspapers

		Globe and Mail %	Toronto Sun %	Toronto Star %	Totals %	N
Primary	News Story	88.9	52.8	64.8	62.6	62
	News Story of Court Case	0.0	5.5	7.4	6.1	6
	News Feature	0.0	2.8	9.3	6.1	6
	Opinion Column	0.0	30.6	7.4	15.1	15
Secondary	Editorials	11.1	5.5	11.1	9.1	9
	Letters to the Editor	0.0	0.0	0.0	0.0	0
	Citizen Opinion Columns	0.0	2.8	0.0	1.0	1
	Col %	100.0	100.0	100.0	100.0	
	N	9	36	54		99
	Row %	9.1	36.4	54.5	100.0	

included in the Toronto Sun were also in the primary news contexts.

The manner in which journalists appeared as sources in these different areas of the newspaper was qualitatively different. In the editorials and opinion columns journalists stated their opinions in a direct manner. In primary news stories journalists typically reiterated "facts" of incidents or cases about attacks on women without acknowledging another source of these "facts". Quite often attributions as to the locus of the problem were embedded in these re-statements of "facts", especially attributions we have interpreted as being directed at the victim.

We have not included a table on "participants" in attacks on women incidents as sources because only 22 were cited as giving the locus of the problem (see Table 3:2). The participants, both victims and offenders, appeared most often in news stories of court cases where they were generally depicted as blaming each other. There are legal constraints on news organizations regarding what they can report about the participants at various stages of the law enforcement and adjudication process (Robertson, 1981), and it is during the public court trial that there is more freedom in citing statements from the offenders and victims.

Summary

The Toronto Star and Toronto Sun gave considerable play to the attacks on women theme over the six month period, averaging about one news item each day that included attributions regarding the problem. The Globe and Mail gave it considerably less attention, averaging about two news items each week that included attributions regarding the problem. When the Globe and Mail did include such items, they tended to cite authorized knowers, including police, criminal justice officials, experts, and official organization representatives, with very few citations from individual citizens. In contrast, the Toronto Star and Toronto Sun not only cited these authorized knowers extensively, but also individual citizens. One explanation for this difference is that the Globe and Mail is directed at a business and professional audience who are mainly interested in official and expert opinion, while the Toronto Sun seeks the popular appeal of "the person in the street", and the Toronto <u>Star</u> as a mass market newspaper also has considerable interest in conveying the "vox pop". Among the sources cited giving accounts of the locus of the problem, police and criminal justice officials were cited in primary contexts in the vast majority of instances; individual citizens appeared mainly in letters columns and primary news stories; experts and organzational representatives appeared mainly in primary news items, although the Toronto <u>Star</u> also included many in secondary news features; and, journalists offered statements related to the problem not only in the secondary news contexts of editorials and opinion columns which they reserve for themselves, but also in primary news contexts. There was not substantial variation among the three newspapers in terms of where various sources were used to convey their accounts of the attacks on women problem.

We now further our analysis by an examination of the nature of accounts regarding attacks on women, and which sources were cited by journalists as offering different accounts.

CHAPTER FOUR

ACCOUNTING FOR ATTACKS ON WOMEN

News Accounts as Ideological Work

News workers, including both journalists and their sources, are involved in ideological work. They collectively constitute "working ideologies" that allow them to accomplish their tasks in a routine and acceptable manner. In this context, ideology is appropriately defined as a framework for knowing that is grounded in a particular mode of existence (newswork) that is also a means not to know (Chibnall, 1977; Fishman, 1978; Tuchman, 1978). Ideology, as a "framework of concepts and values", structures the meaning of an event by providing the background assumptions used to understand what is to be treated as an event, what constitutes fact, and interpretation of that fact. Ideology also enables assessment of an event (for example as legitimate or illegitimate, as a result of certain processes, as similar to other events, and so on).

This does not mean that social knowledge becomes programmed into a unitary discourse. Rather, there are a number of discourses which are continually being tried, sustained, and ruled out. The news media are a major site for this ideological work, assigning social relations to their classifying schemes and contexts. A large part of this work entails designations of what is normal and acceptable and what is deviant, with attendant attributions concerning the nature of problems of deviance and what should be done about them.

> [A]ssignment of social relations to their classifying schemes and contexts is, indeed, the site of an enormous ideological labour, of ideological work: establishing the 'rules' of each domain, actively ruling in and ruling out certain realities, offering the maps and codes which mark our territories and assign problematic events and relations to explanatory contexts,

> helping us not simply to <u>know</u> <u>more</u> about
> 'the world' but to <u>make</u> <u>sense</u> <u>of</u> <u>it</u>. Here,
> the line, amidst all its contradictions, in
> conditions of struggle and contradictions,
> between preferred and excluded explanations
> and rationales, between permitted and
> deviant behaviours, between the
> 'meaningless' and the 'meaningful', between
> the incorporated practices, meanings and
> values and oppositional ones, is
> ceaselessly drawn and redrawn, defined and
> negotiated: indeed, the 'site and stake'
> of struggle (Hall, 1979:341) (emphasis in
> original).

This labour entails a continuing dialectic between the dominant ideologies in the culture and the occupational ideologies of newsworkers. This process, along with aspects of social organization (see Chapter One), frames within a narrowed range what will be reported as a public problem and how that problem will be accounted for. A dominant "consensual paradigm" (Young, 1981) persists, conveying a particular world view. Accounts of the locus of the problem that fall outside the boundaries of this world view are still represented in the news media, but to a limited degree, and when they do appear they are typically presented as eccentricities that all right thinking people can ignore (Tuchman, 1978).

In keeping with the research literature on a variety of "moral panics" (Cohen and Young 1973, Chibnall 1977, Hall <u>et</u> <u>al</u>. 1978, Ng 1981), it is probable that media representation of attacks on women will be embedded in a consensual world view. To summarize this view, the society as presently constituted is the best that citizens can hope for: there is a consensus in terms of values and ideals, including condemnation of violence. Attacks on women, within the consensual world view, is not a phenomenon that is an inevitable outcome of the ways in which this particular society is structured; rather, it is easily explicable in terms of individual or organizational problems: the victim's carelessness, the offender's pathology, the police department's inefficiency, inadequate legislation, etc. The dominant culture which shapes particular attitudes toward women, which permeates the way women are portrayed, and which may ultimately contribute to attacks on women, remains largely unquestioned and unexamined.

The consensual paradigm is reinforced by the working ideology of newsworkers, two important aspects of which are "personalization" and "simplification" as outined in the last chapter. Personalization entails emphasis on those theories which attribute violence, and deviance in general, to factors such as individual pathology, parental failure, or the bad influence of undesirable media output. Relatively excluded or undercut is theorizing related to wider undesirable social conditions or processes. This orientation is reflective of the dominant ideology, which stresses individualism, as well as the criminal law itself, which is also based on individualistic assumptions. Resisted are accounts which suggest people's actions may be attributable to structural inequality and structural forces beyond their control which would diminish or negate their individual responsibility. On the control side of deviance, there is a stress on the deterrent and repressive value of social controls rather than on large scale programs of social reform and reorganization (Chibnall 1977, Young 1981). This is dramatically evidenced, for example, by contemporary crusades against people who drive under the influence of alcohol (Gusfield, 1981).

These considerations also intersect with simplification. News reports tend to oversimplify, glossing the subtle complexities of motivation and situation. Matters are typically reduced to binary oppositions, such as "good" versus "bad" (Chibnall, 1977).

Another consideration is the fact that different newspaper organizations have their own sense of newsworthiness as it relates to their own sense of readership. Each newspaper adopts a characteristic mode of address, a particular language form into which any particular item can be coded; again, this is related to the readership the newspaper perceives itself to be addressing. Newspapers thereby acquire their respective "social personalities". Hall et al. (1978) argue that although there are different newspapers, each with a somewhat distinct "social personality" and "public idiom" (the newspaper's version of the audience that it is principally addressing), this vast range of pluralistic voices being heard is kept within distinct ideological limits. The result is "acknowledgements of order" (Hall, 1979) that are collectively produced.

> Although we have stressed here the different languages this emphasis should not be taken too far. It is not the vast range of voices which the media are sometimes held to represent, but a range within certain distinct ideological limits. While each paper may see itself as addressing a different section of the newspaper-reading public (or different types of newspapers will be in competition for different sectors of the public), the 'consensus of values' which is so deeply embedded in all the forms of public language is more limited than the variety of the forms of public 'language in use' would suggest. (Hall et al., 1978:61) (emphasis in original).

This suggests that accounts of the problem of attacks on women are likely to be within a limited range. Attacks on women will be understood primarily as resulting from the actions of particular individuals, or through its effects on others, not as a result of wider social processes or structures. Moreover, there is unlikely to be a wide divergence in accounts of the locus of the problem among the three newspapers, although who is called upon to do the accounting -- for example, expert and organizational "authorized knowers" as opposed to individual citizens -- may vary somewhat. As we now proceed to document, this is what we discovered in the three newspapers studied as they accounted for the attacks on women problem.

Locating the Problem

In Table 4:1 we present all attributions regarding the locus of the problem in the three newspapers during the six month period under study.

TABLE 4:1

LOCUS OF THE PROBLEM

Locus of the Problem

	Globe and Mail %	Toronto Sun %	Toronto Star %	Totals %	N
Victim	39.2	45.4	50.9	47.1	285
Offender	17.6	15.8	16.2	16.2	98
Criminal Justice System and Policing	16.2	24.4	17.0	20.2	122
Portrayal of Women	10.8	7.2	5.3	6.7	41
Social Pathology	16.2	7.2	10.6	9.8	59
Col %	100.0	100.0	100.0	100.0	
Total N	74	266	265		605
Row %	12.2	44.0	43.8	100.0	

df = 8   p< .10 x^2 = 14.3

Among the 605 attributions, 285 or 47% related to the victim. This is by far the largest category. This is to be understood in the context of the way in which we defined this category. As outlined in Chapter Two, this category includes the many instances in which journalists or their sources repeated circumstances surrounding incidents of attacks on women in ways which suggested that if the victim had taken care not to place herself in perilous circumstances she could have avoided victimization. There was not a substantial difference among the newspapers in the proportionate extent to which the victim was indicated as a locus of the problem.

The offender was identified as the locus of the problem in 98/605, or 16%, of instances. This is perhaps surprising given the view in the research literature that individual pathology is a preferred reading of journalists and their sources, and indeed, an accepted view within the criminal justice system itself. The three newspapers included this type of attribution in almost identical proportions.

There were 122 attributions, or 20%, regarding some aspect of the criminal justice system and policing. These attributions essentially located the problem in organizational mismanagement, e.g. the police were not effective in deterring crime or in solving crime, the courts were not tough enough in sentencing, and the correctional system was unable to rehabilitate offenders. Explicitly or implicitly, this attribution entailed a call for more police and criminal justice resources, reorganization of aspects of the criminal justice system, and law reform and sentencing in the direction of greater punishment. The reporting of crime waves seems to call forth as a "common stock of knowledge" that the problem and solution lies in more formal control (Hall, et al., 1978). This is central to law and order ideology, pressing the belief that more will work where less has not (see generally Rothman, 1980). In this connection it is significant that a popular newspaper such as the Toronto Sun, which seems to traffic in a law and order ideology as a significant part of its trade, had only a marginally greater proportionate inclusion of this attribution than did the other two newspapers.

The remaining types of attributions regarding the locus of the problem were infrequently cited. There were 41 attributions, or just less than 7%, that suggested the problem was connected to the way in which women are portrayed in various media. Again, on a proportionate basis there was little difference among the newspapers in the inclusion of this attribution. About half of the portrayal of women attributions were references to pornography as a "causal" or "linked" phenomenon to the "increase" in attacks on women. Most of the remaining items in the portrayal of women category were specific criticisms of the Toronto Sun and Toronto Star, and were included in letters to the editor columns. The criticisms concerned photographs of women in these newspapers which were deemed by the critics to negatively portray women. As considered in more detail below, most of these critiques were in response to a page in the Toronto Star (July 3, 1982:A3) which juxtaposed photographs of beauty contest candidates with a major story on a rape victim; and, a similar practice in the Toronto Sun whereby news accounts within the attacks on women theme were sometimes juxtaposed with the daily "Sunshine Girl" photograph.

Attributions which we have summarized as "social pathology" were included 59 times, representing about 10% of the total. This category includes attributions which did question wider structural features of the society, and which drew links between these features and the attacks on women phenomenon. The three main structural problems identified were gender relations (16 attributions, e.g. "alienation" between men and women, patriarchy), race relations (16 attributions, all related to one incident in which an attack on a woman was deemed by various sources to have been anti-semitic in its origins or motivation), and public apathy (14 attributions, e.g. a breakdown of community, increased social distance). Among the other 13 social pathology attributions, 5 said the problem was somehow linked to the bad state of the economy. In proportion to the various attributions they included, the Globe and Mail was slightly more likely to have social pathology attributions than were the other two newspapers. However, again there was not a marked difference among the newspapers.

In general, the range of accounts regarding the locus of the problem and their proportionate use was quite similar in all three newspapers. Moreover, a critical discourse outside the dominant paradigm -- either attacking a sign and instrument of women's repression such as pornography, or wider structural pathologies in society - constituted only a minor proportion of attributions. Thus, the consensual paradigm view and its implications, as described at the beginning of this chapter, seems to be evident in the case of the attacks on women moral panic under study. Obviously, wider structural and critical accounts were given some attention. However, these accounts were often undercut by particular journalistic practices, which we shall consider later in presenting aspects of individual news items.

Source Accounts of the Locus of the Problem

The boundaries of legitimate discourse, and acknowledgements of consensus, in news portrayals of public problems are constructed by mobilizing the accounts of sources. It is therefore important to consider what source types are used to convey particular "preferred" accounts of the locus of the problem, and how this might vary among newspapers. As we have previously stated, and shall continue to emphasize and document further, the range of accounts of attacks on women was circumscribed, but who was called upon to provide them varied somewhat among the newspapers studied.

In Table 4:2 we consider the 125 attributions regarding the locus of the problem that were made by police and criminal justice system sources. Over three-quarters of attributions were to the victim. This can be acounted for by appreciating that this source type in general, and the police in particular, are called upon to reiterate the circumstances surrounding crime incidents, the description of which suggests that had victims behaved otherwise (e.g. not taken a shortcut, not used public transit late at night, not been alone in public late at night, etc.) the incident would not have occurred. In a related way, the police are also called upon to recommend crime prevention strategies. It is as "obvious" for them to tell women to take precautions against putting themselves in circumstances such as those cited above as it is for them to tell break and enter victims to buy more and better locks. This leads to a "blaming the victim" preferred reading from these sources, and emphasis upon "victim responsibility" in recommending solutions for controlling the problem.

TABLE 4:2

POLICE AND CRIMINAL JUSTICE SYSTEM SOURCES

AND THE LOCUS OF THE PROBLEM

Police and Criminal Justice System Sources

Locus of the Problem

	Newspaper				
	Globe and Mail %	Toronto Sun %	Toronto Star %	Totals %	N
Victim	65.0	85.1	72.4	76.0	95
Offender	15.0	10.6	24.1	17.6	22
Criminal Justice System and Policing	5.0	4.3	0.0	2.4	3
Portrayal of Women	0.0	0.0	0.0	0.0	0
Social Pathology	15.0	0.0	3.4	4.0	5
Col %	100.0	100.0	100.0	100.0	
Total N	20	47	58		125
Row %	16.0	37.6	46.4	100.0	

As might be expected, police and criminal justice officials were also called upon to depict criminal offenders as a locus of the problem; this was the second most frequently cited attribution from this source type in all three newspapers, although relatively infrequent compared with attributions to the victim.

There was virtually no self-criticism cited for this source type in the form of attributing the problem to inadequacies in their own system. The Toronto Star had no attribution, the Globe and Mail only one, and the Toronto Sun only two, from police and other criminal justice system officials regarding system deficiencies in respect to the problem. One might have expected more arguments about such things as resource deficiencies, inadequate legislation, lenient sentencing, etc. from those within the system as a means of justifying more resources and a greater "crackdown". Contrary to some criminological thought the police and other criminal justice officials did not pick up on others' criticisms of their operations and the general climate of the moral panic to sustain arguments for greater resources. Again, their law and order discourse was largely that of crime prevention via victim precaution, either indirectly by being used to cite circumstances of attacks on women incidents or directly by advising women to avoid these circumstances.

Police and criminal justice system sources were not cited in any newspaper as attributing the problem to the portrayal of women, and there were only five citations regarding social pathology. In sum, to an extensive and very uniform degree, these sources were cited within the discourse of the criminal justice system itself: crime prevention and control through attributing problems to victims' actions, with implied or recommended remedies to induce victim "responsibility"; and, to a much lesser extent, crime prevention and control through attributing problems to the pathological state of offenders, with implications for responsibility and what must be done to contain the "dangerous".

As documented previously, individual citizens were not a preferred source of the Globe and Mail regarding the attacks on women problem.

Among 216 individual citizens' attributions regarding the locus of the problem in the three newspapers, only 10 or less than 5% were in the Globe and Mail. In contrast the "vox pop" orientation of the Toronto Sun probably explains why that newspaper included 115 accounts of the problem from individual citizens. The mass market Toronto Star also appealed to the citizen attributions with relative frequency, totalling 91 attributions.

TABLE 4:3

INDIVIDUAL CITIZENS AND THE LOCUS OF THE PROBLEM

Individual Citizens

Locus of the Problem

Newspaper

	Globe and Mail %	Toronto Sun %	Toronto Star %	Totals %	N
Victim	30.0	38.3	45.0	40.7	88
Offender	30.0	14.8	5.5	11.6	25
Criminal Justice System and Policing	30.0	26.1	27.5	26.9	58
Portrayal of Women	10.0	13.9	9.9	12.0	26
Social Pathology	0.0	6.9	12.1	8.8	19
Col %	100.0	100.0	100.0	100.0	
Total N	10	115	91		216
Row %	4.6	53.2	42.1	100.0	

The most frequently cited locus of the problem from individual citizens was the victim. These attributions frequently appeared in news stories or features in which the reporters adopted a "fear and loathing" angle by interviewing individual women about their reaction to the problem. The Globe and Mail did not report this type of story, but the other two newspapers did so on several occasions.

The "fear and loathing" approach is a means of keeping the theme "alive" and of "personalizing" it to "bring it home" to the reader. Reported interviews were conducted with women asking them of their fears and the precautions that they were taking to deal with the danger. The types of precautions these women were reported to be taking had implicit within them attributions to the victim as a possible locus of the problem. For example, a statement such as "right now, with all the rapes and murders, I'm so nervous I don't even use the TTC after dark" (Toronto Star July 8, 1982:D1) suggests that if one avoids using the Toronto Transit Commission service after dark one can avoid being attacked; by implication women who are attacked after using the TTC late at night contribute to their own fate.

The accompanying story with the headline, "Fear Stalks Metro Women after Cheerleader's Slaying" is of the fear and loathing mode. Individual women are cited as saying they are fearful of going out alone and this is described as being a "state" or condition of city women. All city women have become "victims", their victimization consisting of "fear, insecurity and loss of freedom", following the murder of a respectable woman. Women are said to be "crippled by fear". The dehabilitation is extreme for some. One interviewee wanted her address and workplace kept out of the newspaper "for fear someone would stalk her too". Among 25 women who were reported as having been surveyed, only 3 said they were not scared, and they are reported as saying they would be scared if they listened to the radio or read the newspapers. The other 22 were reported as unanimous in being "tormented by fear for themselves and/or their daughters. They said they're taking all sorts of precautions at night, if they go out at all". "Precautions" included swinging an umbrella like a baseball bat as the person proceeds down the street; putting keys between clenched fingers "in preparation for an

TORONTO STAR, THURSDAY, JUNE 3, 1982/A3

Fear stalks Metro women after cheerleader's slaying

By Patricia Hluchy Toronto Star

Deborah Cornell, 21, won't go out alone at night unless she can take her parents' car or a taxi.

Jill Rorai, 19, is in the same state.

Other young women, who have their own or their family's cars, stay in them honk the horn until their parents come out to the curb to escort them inside.

These women are among probably thousands of Metro women who are victims of fear, insecurity and loss of freedom following Jenny Isford's slaying.

The Star interviewed 25 women in North York, Scarborough and downtown Toronto yesterday to find out how Isford's death by strangulation last Friday has affected them.

Crippled by fear

Twenty-two said they are tormented by fear for themselves and/or their daughters. They said they're taking all sorts of precautions for protection at night, if they go out at all.

The other three said the death had little impact on them only because they never read the paper or listen to the radio, in order to avoid hearing or reading something that could scare them.

"You'd better believe it affected me," said 21-year-old Cornell, who lives and works within six blocks of where Isford's nearly nude body was found, just five doors from her parents' home in the Bayview Ave.-Sheppard Ave. E. area.

Cornell insisted that her address and place of work be withheld if her name was going to be mentioned in The Star, for fear that someone would stalk her too.

'Lunatic out there'

"I can't go out by myself at night; it scares you to think a lunatic was out there doing that. If I go out, I make sure someone's with me right up to my door."

Cornell works in a boutique and her shift sometimes lasts until 9.30 p.m. Before Isford's murder Cornell would sometimes take the bus to her parents' home alone. Now she insists on going with a friend, borrows the family car or takes a taxi.

Like most of the North York women The Star interviewed, Cornell was shocked that such a crime could occur in her affluent, park-like neighborhood, which had always seemed to be immune to the crime of downtown.

"You walk the streets at night, you walk the dog, you think it's a safe neighborhood I was in shock. What if it was me? You hear about it happening downtown, but not up here.

"You feel a little bit of anger because that just shouldn't happen. Why do we have to be so careful now, when before we could be so casual? You're uptight, you're tense; you don't relax as much."

Another 30-year-old North York woman who asked her name not be used said she never considered her vulnerability until last week.

MIKE SLAUGHTER/TORONTO STAR

Playing safe: Deborah, left, and Eva are two of many Metro women who say they won't walk home alone at night since Jennifer Isford was strangled. They say they're now taking all sorts of safety precautions.

"One night I went home at quarter to 12 and had to walk six blocks down dark, residential streets, in a neighborhood similar to the one where she was killed," she said.

"I took my umbrella and swung it back and forth in front of me like a baseball bat. I'm sure I looked like a lunatic but I didn't care."

"It's constantly on my mind," said 19-year-old Jill Rorai, who works in a restaurant in Bayview Village, just a few blocks from where Isford was killed. "Everybody is coming up and saying, 'Make sure you don't walk home anymore'."

Rorai sometimes used to walk the few blocks to her parents' home when her shift ended at midnight or 1 a.m.

Hitches a ride

Now she hitches a ride from one of her bosses or a friend. Like many of the young women without cars whom The Star interviewed, Rorai would like to take taxis home at night, but simply can't afford them.

Kevin Thompson, an evening dispatcher for A-Kwik Taxi in the Yonge St.-Sheppard Ave. area, said calls for taxis have increased dramatically in the past week, although he wasn't sure this was because of calls from fearful women.

"It's been a lot busier this week than it has been for the last month and a half. Monday and Tuesday were the busiest it's been since winter."

In some ways the fallout of Isford's death is worse for mothers, who don't have the youthful fearlessness of their daughters and are often worried sick Friday and Saturday nights until their girls come home.

'Very concerned'

"I've been very concerned for my daughter," said Mary Bryant, who has one daughter, 19-year-old Lisa, still at home and lives close to where Isford died.

"You keep cautioning her. I don't think she'll come off the bus anymore without calling us first. You think if there are houses there, you're safe, but you're obviously not, are you?"

Single mother Holly Kramer, 24, who works in a newsstand at Scarborough Town Centre, says the Isford killing is forcing her to cut back her activity in all sorts of ways. That includes outings with her 3-year-old Caroline.

"I want to take my daughter to Centre Island and I'm trying to figure out how I'm going to go down there and come home before dark. I'll have to go at 6 a.m."

Some women said that when they do have to go out alone at night, they carry their keys between their clenched fingers in preparation for an attacker.

Others said that although they don't believe a woman "invites" an attacker by dressing provocatively, they intend to conceal their evening clothes with a coat when they go out at night on public transit, just to feel less vulnerable.

attacker"; and going to a public park at "6:00 a.m." in order to have enjoyment before dark (this was early June, when nightfall comes about 9:00 p.m.). The fear ramifies to mothers, "who don't have the youthful fearlessness of their daughters and are often worried sick Friday and Saturday nights until their girls come home." The item is complete with a representational photograph of model women who were, in the words of the caption, "playing safe".

Returning to Table 4:3, we find that the second most frequently cited attribution of the problem from individual citizens was policing and the criminal justice system. This was cited 58 times in the three newspapers, or 27% of all attributions of individual citizens. Again the Globe and Mail was not a significant user of the individual citizen to offer this accounting, while the other two newspapers were almost even in their use of citizens to attribute problems to policing and the criminal justice system. This is consistent with conveying popular ideology regarding law and order: the recommendation implicit in saying that the criminal justice system is inadequate was typically to argue that more doses (of law, personpower, punishment, etc.) would work where less had not.

Individual citizens were relatively rarely cited as offering offender pathology, the portrayal of women, or social pathology accounts for attacks on women. Since offender pathology is a common explanatory framework for crime that is legitimate within the criminal process itself, as well as in popular culture (cf. Garofalo, 1981), it is somewhat surprising that less that 12% of attributions cited from individual citizens were of this type. Indeed, attributions more outside the conventional discourse of law and order talk -- including those pertaining to the portrayal of women and to wider social structural problems -- were about as frequently forthcoming from individual citizens as attributions regarding the offender.

However, in focusing upon the portrayal of women attribution, we can consider how this type of critical discourse was allowed to enter the thematic agenda. It entered largely as a means of stimulating debate and keeping the theme alive, and as a means of editorial undercutting of such attributions to make them seem somewhat unreasonable, unacceptable, and not legitimate.

On several occasions the Toronto Sun juxtaposed a news report related to some particular occurrence of an attack on a woman with a picture of their "Sunshine Girl". The Toronto Star used the same technique, including on one occasion an article giving detailed accounts of the physical state of a hospitalized woman who had been raped and assaulted while sunbathing in a park, juxtaposed with an article concerning a bikini contest conducted by a local radio station, complete with pictures of four contestants (see the accompanying article, "Rape Victim may never Recover" on pgs. 58-59).

The editors may have used this particular juxtaposition to encourage readers to think about the societal contradiction of treating women as objects of beauty vis-a-vis brutal attacks on women, and to draw the link between portrayal of women and attacks on women. In any event, this particular page layout had the effect of generating letters to the editor from individual citizens who argued that portrayal of women in beauty contests and news photographs of this type perpetuate treating women as objects and precipitates violence against women. Three letters were published six days after this page was published, followed by two further letters eleven and twelve days later. Thus, the editors created the prospect for individual citizens to write letters with a portrayal of women locus to the problem, and this served to sustain the thematic agenda and issues and debates surrounding it. These five letters accounted for over one-third of all attributions to the portrayal of women in the Toronto Star. Another four letters from individual citizens regarding the portrayal of women, but not related to the particular page layout described above, were also published in the Toronto Star. In sum, when this particular locus of the problem was included in this newspaper, it was largely reserved for the individual opinion of citizens in the particular news context reserved for this purpose.

The same trend is apparent in the Toronto Sun, in which 14/19 attributions to the portrayal of women were made by individual citizens in the letters to the editor column. However, in the case of the Toronto Sun this attribution was not only largely reserved for the letters to the editor news context and individual citizen opinion, it was also undercut by editorial comment after each letter. In each of the fourteen letters appearing in this newspaper's letters to the editor column that identified the portrayal of women as a possible locus of the problem, an editorial comment dismissed such a possibility. The following examples are illustrative.

> The impact of a picture is unquestioned. T.V., newspapers, magazines know this. The impact of the picture of your SUNshine Girl is also unquestioned...but that impact is negative and destructive. Would you have the moral courage to delete this page from your newspaper in view of the reported sickening attacks on young girls in recent weeks?
>
> Editorial Comment - It's sheer rubbish to connect photos with murders. (Toronto Sun, Aug. 6 1982:10)

. . . .

> I find your paper most explicit, almost to the point where it makes me feel ashamed as a women. Surely, in today's society where we have so much violence going on do you not think that perhaps a paper such as yours puts ideas in the minds of some weaklings in our metropolis city? Is there nothing at all to be left to the imagination?
>
> Editorial Comment - It obviously puts ideas in your mind. (Toronto Sun, Aug. 29 1982:10)

★ TORONTO STAR, SATURDAY, JULY 3, 1982/A3

Rape victim may never recover

Attacker smashed her skull in with a brick

By Ellie Tesher Toronto Star

Doctors don't know yet whether a 23-year-old Toronto woman will ever recover from a brutal rape and beating in High Park Wednesday.

The tall, slim, blonde woman is lying in a coma in Toronto General Hospital following the savage attack that smashed a portion of her skull.

She was sunbathing in late morning when a man dragged her to a secluded area, raped and pounded her on the head with a brick.

On Thursday night, she was rushed to an operating room for surgery to relieve pressure on her brain from swelling caused by the blows that fractured the front of her skull.

A team of neurosurgeons is monitoring her condition in the hospital's intensive care unit, checking reflexes of her pupils, corneas, and limbs to assess her brain function.

She is under 24-hour nursing care, hooked up to monitors checking her heart, breathing and blood pressure. Surgeons have drilled a hole in her skull and inserted measuring devices to gauge brain swelling.

It will take at least four days before the severity of her brain injury is known.

The woman, who shared an apartment with two friends in an old, low-rise Bloor St. building across the road, was sunbathing in an open northwest area of the park when her attacker dragged her into a nearby ravine.

Though the park was busy with playing children and summer sun-seekers, no one responded to her screams.

The woman's coma could be the result either of drug treatment to rest her brain and prevent her from resisting the monitoring tubes and needles, or of the massive blow to her head, a hospital spokesman told The Star.

"Right now, they're trying to keep her as stable as possible. It's unknown whether she has brain damage and whether her injury is irreparable," the spokesman said.

Doctors cannot operate on brain swelling. They can only relieve pressure or remove bone to allow more space for the swelling.

"Raised inter-cranial pressure can kill you. Or it can destroy brain tissue and lead to an indefinite coma," a neurosurgeon told The Star.

Metro police on the case yesterday found a second possible weapon that could have smashed the woman's skull.

A blood-stained stone — about the size of a man's fist — was found in the wooded thicket they believe to be the scene of the rape.

Blonde hairs were matted to the stone. Similar hairs were on a blood-splattered brick discovered in the area by police the day before.

"There's a good chance he (the attacker) had the rock and the brick in each hand," Staff Inspector Colin Pitts of 11 Division said.

Police also have some clothes — including a bathing suit they believe belonged to the woman — that they found in the ravine.

Yesterday, a team of more than a dozen officers combed the Bloor-Keele Sts.-High Park area following every possible lead on the assailant.

When the bleeding woman staggered out of the park after the attack, she was barely coherent.

She told police the man who assaulted her first asked her name as she lay sunbathing. She told him to go away.

Police are checking for any connection between the High Park rape beating and the recent sex murders of cheerleader Jenny Isford and nanny Christine Prince.

"We don't think it's connected — there's no solid evidence — but we're looking at it. Just as we're looking at rapes in other divisions," Sgt. Bruce Godfrey said.

Staff Sgt. James Cole, who heads the criminal investigation unit, said police talked to the victim's family and roommates after the attack.

"She's a girl with an impeccable reputation. She comes from a real good family. It's a bad, brutal rape," he said.

Legal fight ahead for father in baby deal

The Metro father of a baby born to a U.S. surrogate mother this week faces a lengthy court battle before he can legally call the boy his son.

Frank Drea, minister of community and social services, says the man must "prove" he is the natural father before he'll have any legal claim to the baby.

In the meantime, Metro Toronto Catholic Children's Aid Society has taken legal charge of the baby and will ask the courts Monday for an interim care and custody order.

Hospital officials asked the society to step in because they were "wary of releasing the child into hands unknown," Drea said.

The baby was born in Toronto hospital June 26 and will be kept there until the courts award the agency a custody order.

The unnamed natural mother, who is married and has a child of her own, returned to Florida the day after the baby was born.

She had originally been paid $10,000 for her services, but returned the money after Drea hinted the government had legal means to block the deal.

The court case on Monday involves only the transfer of custody issue.

"Adoption is a long way down the road," Drea said.

He said the matter is complicated by the fact the insemination took place in the U.S.

"The difficulty is going to be that all these people are still in the United States — I don't know if they want to come here."

The surrogate mother's lawyer, Noel Keane of Dearborn, Mich., would be helpful in eventually settling the matter, Drea said.

"But if he sets foot in Canada, he'll be arrested. He tried to sell a baby."

Drea said he doubts the mother would

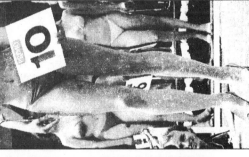

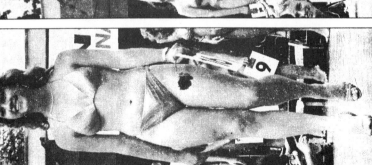

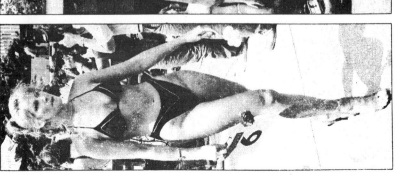

Oh, la, la: Metro weather warmed up this week just in time to allow the Miss CHIN-Bikini Pageant to proceed without goosebumps. Among those in yesterday's pre-view were, from left, Una Fawns, 22, of Richmond Hill; Linda Terry, 17, of Brampton; Tracy Zechna, 16, of Brampton; and Karen Golden, 19, of Toronto. Finals are to take place this afternoon at 2 at the Canadian National Exhibition. Miss CHIN-Bikini's prizes include a Mercury LN7 car. **Other picnic stories/A10.**

KEITH BEATY/TORONTO STAR

The findings that these abuses of women
relate to viewing pornographic materials by
the perpetrator is valid. I agree that a
stop should be put to materials that
portray women as creatures who enjoy every
bit of the violation of their bodies. The
concepts these smut magazines brings across
trigger barbaric behaviour towards the
female sex

Editorial Comment - The so-called findings
are utterly meaningless. (Toronto Sun,
Aug. 20 1982:10)

. . . .

Re Argo Sunshine squad's first performance
(Sun, June 13): "A few flinched at the
comments from boys draped over the rails".
Well, girls, boys become men...and your
T.A. routines are helping to define women
as teasing, Barbi-doll victims. "We did it
for Jenny". You surely did and now you're
doing it for me and every other woman.
Please stop advertising what isn't for
sale. You put us all in danger.

Editorial Comment - Nonsense. (Toronto
Sun, June 23 1982:10).

The authors of these letters identify not only the portrayal of
women as a possible locus of the problem, but in the first two also
point an accusing finger at the Toronto Sun for contributing to such a
portrayal. The editorial comments are dismissive of the reasoning, the
first, third and fourth by directly attacking the theorizing, and the
second by undercutting the letter writer.

One might question why the Toronto Sun allowed for such views to be
expressed at all. Hall et al. (1978) have argued one of the main
functions of the letters to the editor column is to stimulate
controversy, provoke public response and further "debate". This
certainly did occur in the present instance not only by publishing the
above letters but also letters which refuted portrayal of women
theorizing; not surprisingly, the editorial comments pertaining to

these letters were in agreement with the letter writers' reasoning. Another function of letters columns is to increase the newspaper's legitimacy (the idea of a free press) by making it appear that its pages are open to views that the editorial collective may not adhere to (ibid). In the present instance these views may have been expressed but they were certainly not given the same type of treatment as more "acceptable views". Thus, it is reasonable to conclude that the inclusion of these letters was one vehicle by which the newspaper effected its own preferred reading, and ultimately, ideological closure. Erikson (1966) has argued that media coverage of crime and deviance serves to demarcate the boundaries of what is aceptable behaviour. It can be suggested that the representation of attributions to the portrayal of women served a similar function. By designating these interpretations as deviant or unacceptable the boundaries of what was considered legitimate theorizing on the issue were clearly drawn. In the Toronto Sun this theorizing was used as a vehicle to acknowledge the "normal" and to rule out accounts not in accordance with it.

The Globe and Mail was quite different in this respect. Among eight attributions to the portrayal of women as the locus of the problem, only one came from an individual citizen, and in this instance the citizen cited an academic journal reference to argue the link between pornography and sexual aggression.

More generally, the Globe and Mail did not use the page layout techniques of the other two newspapers to juxtapose case stories of attacks on women with suggestive photographs and stories. In comparison, the other two newspapers, and in particular the Toronto Sun, relied upon "dollops" (RCN 1981a) and made extensive use of the news imperative of titillation. Again, this has implications for circumscribing discourse and for restricting understanding. As Chibnall (1977:33) remarks, "...the commercial imperative of titillation trivializes reality and diverts attention from politics and social problems, substituting superficial salacity for genuine understanding and thus clearing the ground for interpretations of newspaper ideology."

Theorizing about the portrayal of women as the locus of the problem was most likely to come from individual citizens in the Toronto Sun (16/19 of all such attributions) and the Toronto Star (9/14 of all such attributions). However, the Toronto Star did also rely on experts and organizational representatives for making this attribution (5/14), and this source type predominated in the Globe and Mail citations of this attribution (6/8).

TABLE 4:4

EXPERTS AND ORGANIZATIONAL REPRESENTATIVES

AND THE LOCUS OF THE PROBLEM

Experts and Organizational Representatives

Locus of the Problem

	Newspapers				
	Globe and Mail %	Toronto Sun %	Toronto Star %	Totals %	N
Victim	7.1	21.3	17.4	16.5	20
Offender	14.3	23.4	32.6	24.8	30
Criminal Justice System and Policing	28.6	40.4	23.9	31.4	38
Portrayal of Women	21.4	4.3	10.9	10.8	13
Social Pathology	28.6	10.6	15.2	16.5	20
Col %	100.0	100.0	100.0	100.0	
Total N	28	47	46		121
Row %	4.6	53.2	42.1	100.0	

It can be argued that the different status of sources, or their particular "rung" on the "hierarchy of credibility", is also an element in affecting the theorizing about the locus of the problem. Thus, an expert (psychiatrist, sociologist, criminologist, psychologist) cited as drawing a link between the portrayal of women and violence against women, or a representative of a recognized organization doing the same thing, may be taken more seriously than an individual citizen making the same statement. Moreover, there are means to either support or discredit a particular instance of theorizing, e.g. placing particular words in front of the statements of experts to show that they are making a factual statement, while individual citizens may be depicted as making allegations, statements unsupported by evidence, or simply undercut (as were the letter writers to the Toronto Sun regarding the portrayal of women locus of the problem).

The use of experts as authorized knowers often carries the aura of science, along with the socially important organized contexts in which science is produced and communicated. This is indicated by the following exerpts.

> [Setting is a session on pornography and sexual violence at the American Psychiatric Association meeting] Dr. Natalie Shainess, a New York psychoanalyst, called pornography "a serious, destructive force threatening society." She said hard-core pornography contributes to an acceptance of violence and "inures us to brutality" (Globe and Mail May 21, 1982:10)

> Several controlled studies by Neil Malamuth, a psychology professor at the University of Manitoba, suggest that pornography and even depictions of rape and violence against women in T.V. and popular films can make men more callous to the victimization of women. (Toronto Star, July 24, 1982:B4)

Similarly, representatives of established and legitimate organizations are given standing to be heard by other legitimate bodies,

and this standing is conveyed in the news account. For example, a
statement is attributed to a representative from the National Action
Committee on the Status of Women, testifying at a meeting of the Senate
legal affairs comittee.

> Men are encouraged by pornography to
> believe women like being raped, testified
> Miss Ridington. "Given the fact that men
> are constantly bombarded with pornography
> that tells them women really want to be
> raped, any man could claim to believe such
> lies about women" (Globe and Mail, October
> 15 1982:15).

To summarize, critical discourse related to locating the problem
with the portrayal of women received relatively scant attention in each
of the newspapers. However, in the relatively few items in which this
attribution did occur, there was some qualitiative difference among the
newspapers in how it was cited and used. The Toronto Sun mainly cited
individual citizens in their reserved place, the letters to the editor
column, and then undercut their statements with replies from the editor.
The Toronto Star citations of this attribution mainly came from
individual citizens' letters, but in addition they did include the views
of several organizational representatives and experts. The Globe and
Mail tended to cite mainly experts and organizational representatives
regarding the portrayal of women attribution, and the one citizen's
letter containing this attribution cited a scholarly journal article in
support of the causal link being drawn between pornography and attacks
on women. This is again in keeping with the distinctions we have drawn
previously between the "popular" and "quality" press.

The data in Table 4:4, compared with data in Tables 4:2, 4:3, and
4:5, indicate that experts and organizational representatives were the
only source type who did not predominantly give attributions that
located the problem with the victim. These sources gave a fuller range
of accounts regarding the locus of the problem, although with relatively
more emphasis on problems with the police and criminal justice system,

and offender pathology. In terms of newspaper differences in attributions from this type of source, the <u>Globe</u> <u>and</u> <u>Mail</u> included proportionately more attention to portrayal of women and social pathology attributions and less to the offender and victim than the other two newspapers.

Examining the actual sources used in the three newspapers again illuminates some differences among them. As stated in Chapter Three, many of the organizational representatives in the Toronto <u>Star</u> and Toronto <u>Sun</u> were persons representing citizens' groups demanding specific action, and ultimately more law and order (see also Chapter Two for an enumeration of the range of groups cited). These groups often criticized the police or criminal justice system as part of their demands for a "crackdown" on the "dangerous". The two leaders of the Guardian Angels, a New York based group which organizes individuals to patrol city streets, came to Toronto on several occasions during the period of the moral panic, capitalizing on the panic to argue police inefficiency and therefore the need for their brand of public safety. This group received wide media coverage each time they appeared, especially in the Toronto <u>Sun</u> and Toronto <u>Star</u>. The basic news frame contained their arguments about inefficiency and how they could help , followed by responses from the police and other officials. Other groups echoed the calls for law and order as they criticized the criminal justice system as a locus of the problem regarding attacks on women. Again, they were given considerable play, especially in the Toronto <u>Sun</u> and Toronto <u>Star</u>. For example, an organization called Citizens United for Safety and Justice was cited in the Toronto <u>Sun</u> as locating the problem in an allegedly lenient punishment system.

> Victims of Violence are calling for a national referendum on capital punishment and a complete overhaul of the National Parole Board. As well, the group wants the mandatory supervision program -- which allows a prisoner out after two-thirds of a sentence has been served -- abolished. (Toronto <u>Sun</u>, July 14, 1982).

Similarly, the offender pathology attribution was frequently invoked by experts and organizational representatives, especially in the Toronto Star and Toronto Sun, to in effect argue that there were "dangerous" people in the midst of the city's citizens who required more control. The thrust was that the person who suffers from a criminal pathology he is incapable of modifying on his own requires intervention by the authorities. Again, this attribution can function to further arguments about the need for law and order, and the Toronto Sun and Toronto Star cited many representatives of citizen interest organizations attributing the problem to the offender in this vein.

In contrast, the Globe and Mail gave relatively more attention to authorized knowers with standing as experts or as representatives of governmental official organizations. Moreover, their experts focused more on the portrayal of women and social pathology attributions, especially as compared with offender pathology or the victim. Although few in number, their social pathology attributions did occasionally point to major structural factors, as in the following passage with reference to sociologists Joseph Moralla and Diana Scully.

> The way they see it, behavior always communicates a set of beliefs and values. Since there's little doubt that misogny permeates patriarchal society, it seems likely that rapists aren't that abnormal after all. Their behavior may, in fact, just represent an example of a socially-sanctioned continuum of male sexual aggression. (Globe and Mail, June 12 1982:Fanfare 3).

In summary, the Globe and Mail was proportionately much more likely to cite experts and organizational representatives than other source types; and, when it did so it typically used representatives of official organizations or scientific expertise as opposed to representatives of organizations for popular causes or interests as did the other newspapers.

In Table 4:5 we document that when journalists gave information indicating the locus of the problem, it was in the majority of instances in relation to the victim. This is largely the case because of the journalistic practice of repeating circumstances of instances of attacks on women in subsequent stories within the theme, thereby suggesting that if the victim or potential victims avoided such circumstances there would be less of a problem. The only other frequently cited attributions from journalists concerned the police and criminal justice system. This attribution was especially frequent in the Toronto Sun, and again is consistent with that newspaper's emphasis on the problem of a lenient crime control system as one major reason for the problem of attacks on women. This attribution was given 13 times by journalists in the Toronto Sun, and 9 times by journalists in the Toronto Star; in contrast, there were no such attributions from Globe and Mail journalists.

TABLE 4:5

JOURNALISTS AND THE LOCUS OF THE PROBLEM

Journalists
Newspapers

Locus of the Problem

	Globe and Mail %	Toronto Sun %	Toronto Star %	Totals %	N
Victim	80.0	46.7	66.1	60.0	72
Offender	0.0	11.1	9.2	9.2	11
Criminal Justice System and Policing	0.0	28.9	13.8	18.3	22
Portrayal of Women	10.0	2.2	0.0	1.7	2
Social Pathology	10.0	11.1	10.8	10.8	13

		Globe and Mail	Toronto Sun	Toronto Star	Totals	
	Col %	100.0	100.0	100.0	100.0	
Totals	Total N	10	45	65		120
	Row %	80.3	37.5	54.2	100.0	

Summary

In this chapter we began with a discussion of research literature which informs us how news accounts are the product of "ideological work", and that a dominant, consensual paradigm prevails so that certain accounts are systematically included while others are systematically undercut or excluded. The pervasiveness of the dominant culture, as well as occuptional culture news imperatives such as personalization and simplification, explain why there will be similarities among newspapers in the range of accounts of any particular problem. In the present case of an attacks on women moral panic, we indeed found considerable similarity among the three newspapers in the types of attributions made and the relative extent to which these attributions were included. The predominant attributions related 1) to the victim, especially in terms of how victim precautions can serve as a major device for crime prevention; 2) to the criminal justice system, especially how more and improved laws, policing and punishment is another major crime prevention device; and 3) to offender pathology, especially how there is a need to identify and control "dangerous" individuals in society. More critical accounts attributing the problem to the portrayal of women in various media or to wider social structural deficiencies (including aspects of gender relations) received relatively little attention. Moreover, these later accounts were most often from individual citizens in their special place, the letters to the editor column; furthermore, in the Toronto Sun these accounts were routinely undercut by dismissive editorial comment following the letters.

Different sources were cited as giving different relative emphasis to the locus of the problem. Police and criminal justice system officials predominantly underscored the role of the victim as the locus of the problem, paving the way for recommendations that precautions by women were the best means of preventing attacks. Individual citizens also gave the most emphasis to the victim as the locus of the problem. In the main these were women who were cited in news stories or feature articles, expressing fear and relating the precautions they were taking.

The central message was that women were to collaborate in their own control and attendant restrictions on freedom. In the relatively infrequent instances when individual citizens were cited in a more critical discourse, attributing the problem to the portrayal of women, it was not in news stories and features but in letters to the editor columns. Again, at least in the Toronto Sun, these efforts were undercut by dismissive editorial comments following the letters. Experts and organizational representatives were the only source type cited as giving less emphasis to the victim than other attributions. They gave more emphasis to the offender and police and criminal justice system in locating the problem; in the Toronto Star and especially in the Toronto Sun, many of these were representatives of citizens' organizations calling for more and better laws, law enforcement, and punishment of criminals. In the Globe and Mail there were some critical statements from experts regarding portrayal of women and social pathology attributions.

In examining the proportionate citation of sources making attributions regarding the attacks on women problem, and in a more fine-grained analysis of the particular types of sources used within each source category, it is possible to see differences among the three newspapers. Proportionately, the Globe and Mail did rely more on experts and official representatives, and did have a greater range of critical comments about social attitudes and social structure, than the other two newspapers. The Toronto Star had a fuller range of persons within the various source categories providing a fuller range of attributions. The Toronto Sun tended to give particular emphasis to popular ideology related to law and order -- crime prevention, legal system improvement, pursuing the dangerous -- by citing extensively individual citizens as well as representatives of citizens' organizations advocating various law and order measures. There was some variation among the newspapers, although circumscribed within the cultural limits of what would be accepted as legitimate attributions from legitimate source consituencies.

CHAPTER FIVE

DOMINANT IDEOLOGY, IMAGES OF WOMEN
AND THE POLITICS OF LAW AND ORDER

Introduction

In this chapter we summarize our research findings to this point to emphasize that there was little variation among the newspapers in their frameworks for understanding the problem. We then proceed to consider further the process by which attacks on women was made a problem within the public culture (Gusfield, 1981). We examine how the problem developed as part of the politics of law and order (Schur, 1980); that is, how various groups used the opportunity to state their own preferred causal accounts of the problem as a means of furthering their preferred political causes. At least in the newspapers studied, a central image of this politics was that the problem was best controlled by having women take precautions that restricted their freedom. We trace how this "blaming the victim" (Ryan, 1971) view was sustained in news accounts by mobilizing all source types in various news contexts. Beyond this, we suggest how the symbolic politics of this moral panic, of which the news media were an integral part, can be seen as effecting the social control of women. By locating the problem with the victim, and by not questioning the cultural and social structures in general, and gender relations in particular, with a similar frequency or intensity, the news accounts functioned to "acknowledge" (Hall, 1979) the existing order of values and social relations which perpetuate the subordinate place of women.

Ryan (1971) discusses a type of thinking which he terms "blaming the victim". In such thinking it is the victim who needs adjusting while the social institutions and practices which may be responsible for the victim's suffering remain untouched. In the present context, it was the woman victim of the attack who was deemed in need of control over

her behaviour; the social institutions and processes that may have
encouraged attacks, or which may have led them to be regarded lightly,
were given relatively little attention and sometimes dismissed. The
newspapers arguably perpetuated views that it is something women do that
contributes to attacks. This permeated all news contexts. Experts and
organizational representatives were mobilized to offer advice to women
on the precautions they were to adopt; individual citizens in letters to
the editor columns reiterated this advice; "women in the street"
interviewed by the reporters were used to add futher credence to this
image by repeating that advice; and, the primary reports of the
incidents, which focused on the actions of the victim immediately prior
to the attack, provided women with an illustration of what could happen
should they choose not to adopt these precautions.

The journalist as author chooses the questions to ask their
sources, decides which of the many statements their sources offer will
be printed, and decides how to cite sources in the context of the
narrative. For example, the police may provide a number of details
about the event, but the journalist controls what will be reported and
how. As we document in the next section, journalists repeat statements
relating to what the victim was doing immediately prior to the attack,
and reiterate these 'facts' each time the incident is re-told. The
journalist asked individual citizens what precautions they were taking
to avoid attacks, and experts what precautions women should adopt to
avoid attacks. Thus, the image of attacks on women was situated and
presented as a coherent whole, with members of various source
constituencies basically agreeing on the locus of the problem and
attendant remedies.

The dominant representation of attacks on women was situated in
stereotypical notions of gender relations. While critical theorizing on
the subject was presented, paying attention to how structural features
in society may contribute to attitudes, which in turn may lead to
attacks, it was minimal and sometimes discredited. One common criticism

of newspaper reporting of particular issues is that it is all too often separated from news analysis (Smart and Smart, 1978:96). It can be argued that the phenomenon of attacks on women **was analyzed**, but within a particular stereotypical framework, and that this analysis failed to address the socio-economic, historical, and cultural context of which the event is a manifestation.

> Such news reports, rather than generating understanding, or correcting misunderstandings of an event by situating the phenomenon within its socio-cultural context, tend to dwell upon the specific idiosyncratic charateristics of the particular event, trade off and indeed ultimately perpetuate commonly held conceptions or stereotypes of the phenomenon. (Smart and Smart, 1978:94)

The Royal Commission on Newspapers (1981c) categorized the competition among the three major daily newspapers in Toronto as following a 'coexistence' model. Although the three newspapers are in competition with each other, it is understood that they will continue to offer readers a choice and newspapers will vie for only a portion of the readership (ibid:75). There was some diversity in the area of the newspaper where the phenomenon was dealt with, the sources, the locus of the problem, and the qualitative handling of the issue. These differences reflect the different 'social personalities' of the newspapers and their respective readerships. Overall, however, these differences did not reflect substantially different interpretations of the phenomenon. Rather, different sources were mobilized in different news contexts by the three newspapers to give basically the same framework within which to understand the problem. In respect to the coverage of the attacks on women theme, the three newspapers studied appear to add support to recent theorizing which suggests that media organizations present fairly uniform images. We now proceed to present further data on the construction of those images, and to theorize about the implications for the social control of women.

Constituting the Victim as the Locus of the Problem

> The important point about the structured
> relationship between the media and the
> primary institutional definers is that it
> permits the institutional definers to
> establish the initial definition or primary
> interpretation of the topic in question.
> This interpretation then 'commands the
> field' in all subsequent treatment and sets
> the terms of reference within which all
> further coverage takes place...
>
> ...The media, then, do not simply 'create'
> the news; nor do they simply transmit the
> ideology of the 'ruling class' in a
> conspiratorial fashion. Indeed, we have
> suggested that in a critical sense, the
> media are frequently not the 'primary
> definers' of news events at all; but their
> structured relationship to power has the
> effect of making them play a crucial but
> secondary role in reproducing the
> definitions of those who have privileged
> access, as a right, to the media as
> 'accredited sources'. From this point of
> view, in the moment of news production, the
> media stand in a position of structured
> subordination to the primary definers.
> (Hall et al., 1978: 58,59)

The police, as primary institutional definers, were central to
formulating the problem of attacks on women in terms of the victim.
This was done initially by citing police reports of the circumstances
surrounding particular incidents of attacks on women that became part of
the thematic agenda and moral panic. Detailing the circumstances also
conveyed the message that women needed to take precautions to avoid
further incidents. Moreover, explicit advice to women to take
precautions was regularly and frequently repeated by police sources as
the theme unfolded. With the problem so framed, much of the subsequent
discussion by various sources in different news contexts was within the
same frame. In this section we trace the development of this frame
through an examination of news items in the Toronto Star.

On May 29 1982 the front page of the Toronto Star contained a picture of a young woman with a headline, "Friends weep for slain cheerleader" (Toronto Star, May 29 1982:A1). The news story pertaining to this photograph revealed the details of what had happened. It was from this point that the police as primary definers were cited in a way which set up the frame for subsequent discussion of the phenomenon. Homicide detectives were quoted as saying that a man "...attacked her minutes after she got off a bus near her Blithfield Ave. home about 1 a.m. yesterday" (Toronto Star, May 29 1982:A1). This statement was the beginning of the process of attributing the problem to the victim. Within the same news story the police were cited to inform the readers of another incident; "The woman was taking a shortcut on a path through a ravine when she was slashed by a knife-wielding man" (Toronto Star, May 29 1982:A1). The reader is further informed that "...police officers have visited at least two nearby high schools advising students of the dangers of walking home alone at night" (Toronto Star, May 29 1982:A1). Thus, within a single news story we see the structuring of the understanding of the problem within a certain frame. Jenny Isford was murdered after riding the TTC late at night, another woman was attacked after taking a short cut through a ravine, and the police are advising students that it is dangerous to walk home alone at night. Attacks on women occur to those who are not careful. This initial impression was further strengthened in the subsequent news coverage of this case.

That same day the Toronto Star published a news story citing interviews with the victim's friends to capture their reaction to the attack. A comment made by one of these friends further strengthened this initial impression "...but she was 'always cautious - not the kind of girl that would hitchhike or take a ride home with a stranger'" (Toronto Star, May 29 1982:A2). This particular attack was presented as incomprehensible to her friend because she was not the kind of girl who was supposed to be attacked, she was always careful. This type of statement of course has powerful implications for the locus of the

problem. It is "normally" something that a certain "kind" of woman does
that contributes to attack. Panic is heightened if this kind of thing
can happen to "respectable" women in the course of everyday activity,
and it becomes necessary for every woman to take precautions.

Subsequent news stories, particularly those which reported on the
state of the police investigation, continued to strengthen the view of
the victim as the locus of the problem. The facts of the case that had
originally contributed to this dominant image of attacks on women were
reiterated by the journalist without acknowledgements of other sources.
This type of journalistic practice largely accounts for the relatively
high proportion of journalists categorized as sources in news stories.

News stories often contained the description of more than one
incident, which generally added to the strength of this initial
impression. For instance, in one news story four different incidents
were reported.

> The attractive 19-year-old rookie Argo
> cheerleader was strangled just a few feet
> from a Bayview Ave. bus stop and only a few
> doors from her Blithfield Ave. home after
> she got off a northbound bus in the early
> hours of the morning.
>
> Specifically, police are wondering whether
> Jenny's killer is the same man who attacked
> a 19-year-old North York woman May 3 while
> she jogged on Leslie St. just north of
> Sheppard Ave. E.
> The woman was jogging at about 1 a.m. when
> she was pounced on by a husky man who
> dragged her into a ravine and raped
> her...both took place in the early morning.
>
> In one attack, a 29-year-old woman was
> raped after getting off a late night bus in
> the York Mills - Valley Woods Rds. area; in
> the other a 17-year-old girl was stabbed by
> a man while taking a shortcut through a
> ravine in the Bayview Ave. - York Mills Rd.
> area. (Toronto Star, June 1 1982:A6)
> (Emphasis added).

Again, this contributes to the dominant image that women who are attacked are in some way responsible since they did not take the necessary precautionary measures required of them.

Of course, linking isolated occurrences in this manner is central to constituting the thematic agenda and attendant moral panic. Fishman (1978) has argued that during some moral panics the police, for various organizational reasons, may contribute to such perceptions by themselves drawing or implying connections between isolated events. Although the police appeared to have raised the question of a link between cases at the beginning, for example they are reported as suggesting a possible link between the attack on Jenny Isford and the attack on Christine Prince ("Nanny's brutal murder similar to cheerleader's, police believe" Toronto Star, June 23 1982:A1) they later denied the possiblity ("Sex killings of two women not linked, police believe," (Toronto Star, June 24 1982). Furthermore, the police denied that there was any statistical evidence to substantiate the media's claim that there was an increase in violence against women in Toronto, but this wasn't reported in the newspapers (See pp. 12-13). Instead, newspaper coverage of the meeting where this evidence was presented placed a strong emphasis on the precautionary measures that speakers had suggested women adopt. At another point during field research at the Metropolitan Toronto Police Public Affairs department the researcher was told by a police officer that there was no statistical evidence to suggest that there had been any such increase in attacks on women during the summer of 1982 as compared to the summer of 1981.

This draws attention to the fact that the police do not have routine control over the news coverage and attendant moral panic of a crime wave. When occurrences which become police property are routinely passed on to the newspapers, the police tend to lose control over how they will be handled. One way that the police can control the perception of a moral panic is to stop supplying the newspapers with the type of incidents that are the subject of the moral panic. However, reporters may find out about these incidents by other means, and if they do so they would be likely to cast negative commentary on the police for not making them public. Moreover, even if the number of incidents that the newspaper can report is reduced there are other organizations which can be used to keep the theme alive, by suggesting the locus of the problem and what remedies are appropriate. As previously documented, in the context of this particular moral panic many groups were consulted in the public culture marketplace to identify the locus of the problem and to suggest remedies as these reflected political ideologies and interests.

Hall et al. (1978) have argued that secondary news reports tend to provide the answers to the questions implicitly posed in the primary news reports. In this particular instance it appeared rather more like the secondary news reports were reinforcing the answers to the problem which were implicitly given in the primary news reports. Although attributions to the victim were not the most frequent to appear in opinion columns, they did appear, contributing to the overall image of attacks on women that had first been created in the news stories. For example, one columnist stated, "I tell a guy that the dead girl shouldn't have been on the bus alone at that hour, she was taking a chance" (Toronto Star, June 1 1982:A2). "The dead girl" is Jenny Isford.

In the primary reports the police are used by the journalist as part of the emphasis on the 'fact' that Isford had been on a bus, late at night, alone. The consistent reiteration of this 'fact' in effect elevates it to the status of having some causal connection with the attack. As is evident in the opinion column excerpt cited above, the journalist legitimates this new status by also identifying that 'fact' as eminently important within the whole incident. The following excerpt from an editorial further illustrates this tendency.

> And yet the basic reality, too is that even
> the safest of big cities these days are not

> as safe as we would wish - and the
> vulnerable need to govern themselves
> accordingly. We can no longer take for
> granted that it is safe for a woman to walk
> alone along virtually any street of our
> city in the dark of night;...(Toronto Star,
> July 14 1982:A21).

The Toronto Star strengthened this image further in the way it
recruited experts, including police officers as crime prevention
experts, to offer advice to women on how they could protect themselves
against attack. The advice that these sources were reported as offering
added further credence to the original formulation of the problem.

> ...rape experts advise women who work late
> or live alone to use caution and common
> sense. The psychiatrist says though women
> can shop downtown, and walk the city
> streets in daylight, they mustn't allow
> themselves to talk to strange men.
> Especially alone. (Toronto Star, July 6
> 1982:A6) (Emphasis added).

. . . .

> "I was sunbathing by myself in the park
> and a police car pulled up beside me",
> said Rosemarie Halbig, 24. "The officer
> warned me about what happened and said I
> shouldn't be alone in such a secluded
> spot" (Toronto Star, July 2 1982:A3).

. . . .

> Porter (Toronto Transit Commission
> chairman) cautioned riders to follow
> police recommendations when "it comes to
> leaving our system in the late evening
> hours: When walking home alone at night,
> avoid dark, secluded areas; travel in
> pairs, whenever possible; arrange to be
> met at a subway station or bus stop and
> never accept rides from strangers in
> automobiles" (Toronto Star, July 14
> 1982:A1).

It is the media who manufacture the theme and attendant moral panic, as it is built into more than the sum of information supplied by individual sources or source types. Of course, in the manufacturing process sources may also have their views communicated and their interest position served. For example, in their role as sources regarding the attacks on women moral panic the police were able to communicate a basic crime prevention message that the victim should take precautions. As mentioned previously, the police are used by the media to convey a similar message when there are crime waves of other sorts, e.g. after a wave of break and enters, to recommend better security devices to all householders and apartment dwellers. Moreover, such advice is not in itself unreasonable given the very severe limitations on the police in knowing about and solving crimes (cf. Ericson 1981, 1982; Kelling 1983; Punch 1983) and therefore the need for citizens to be directly concerned with crime prevention. The point being made here is that regardless of these considerations as they are communicated in the particular news item, their cumulative effect as they are contextualized in the general news theme is to primarily locate the problem with the victim as a preferred reading, to the relative exclusion of other accounts and their attendant implications for social control and political action. This is underscored by calling upon other sources - from psychiatrists to public transit authorities - to state the same view, and by journalists themselves using editorial and opinion columns to further establish the dominant reading.

Individual citizens, in feature fear and loathing stories and letters to the editor, were also used to squarely establish this frame as not only the most sensible view, but also the most popular one. As Hartley (1982:90) observes, these feature news items "are used to give flavour, reaction, or mood to issues that have been raised in the news...They authenticate the coverage given to particular events by showing the concern of ordinary people in the issue; and they serve as potential points of identification for the audience, who are presumed to share the style and 'widely held opinions' voiced in the vox pop". The dominant locus of the problem offered readers by journalists, police, and other authorized knowers in the primary news reports, features, editorials and opinion columns is also authenticated by the apparent consensus among ordinary folk. This is apparent in the previously cited Toronto _Star_ news feature (p. 54), and in the following excerpts from subsequent Toronto _Star_ items citing individual citizens.

1) No street is safe

> Crimes such as this can be avoided by not travelling alone... (Toronto _Star_, June 12 1982:B3)

. . . .

2) Fear stalks women on the TTC

> Prince, a Welsh-born nanny, disappeared sometime Monday after stepping from a westbound St. Clair Ave. streetcar, shortly after 1.30 a.m., police believe. Jenny Isford...had taken a late night bus...Fagerros who works until 9 p.m., said she purposely avoids going out at night alone unless she has a ride home or a male escort. "My mother tells me not to wear anything flashy on the subway and not to draw attention to myself", said De Vires, who was wearing a plain, baggy track suit, as she waited for her parents to pick her up from a station in North York. (Toronto _Star_, June 25 1982:A6)

. . . .

3) Frightened women travel in pairs after sex attacks

> "I won't take a subway at night. Now I'm even afraid to sunbathe in the day".
> "I try to come home earlier,..."
> (Toronto _Star_, July 8 1982:A3)

. . . .

4) Metro women to TTC: We don't feel safe

"I won't use the subway after 9 o'clock
at night". (Toronto *Star*, July 8
1982:D1).

. . . .

5) Wendy Stirrat will never jog alone
again. Cathy Sirmay used to cut
through the park to get to her
apartment on Bloor St. Now, she won't
walk through alone.

Lillian Duric and her daughter Denise
hurried as they crossed the area where
it happened. "I'll never walk through
here alone", she said. "Nobody would"
(Toronto *Star*, July 14 1982:A4)

. . . .

6) "Lone female jogger is taking a big
risk"

On a recent evening, at approximately
9:30 p.m. I saw a young lady jogging by
herself...until our police department
apprehends these maniacs, a little bit
of common intelligence may possibly
prevent another senseless loss of life.
(Toronto *Star*, July 21 1982:A23)

. . . .

7) Mode of dress must be a factor

I have been reading and hearing so much
about the sex attacks on and rapes of
women in the city of Toronto in the
past few months, through the
newspapers, radio and television - it
seems to be a daily news item.

Not too much seems to be said regarding
the dress or demeanor of some women
while travelling on TTC, on the beach,
and even on the street. Teenagers, in
particular, seem to go as scantily clad
as possible during those hot summer
days, surely mode of dress and actions
are factors in a lot of these attacks.

I think Toronto's Finest are doing a
great job. (Toronto _Star_, July 31
1982:B3).

As our analysis in previous chapters indicates, this was not the
only view of the problem and its remedy conveyed during the six months
under study. However, it was a dominant view, weaved through all
primary and secondary news contexts and involving the mobilization of
all source types, including police and other experts to establish it,
and individual citizens to give it a sense of popular consensus.

Theorizing Implications for the Social Control of Women

What is particularly striking, and requires explanation, is the
extent to which individual women as sources repeated the conception of
the victim as the locus of the problem and reiterated the advice of
authorized knowers to take precautions.

One possible explanation is that the reporter, by asking individual
women sources if they were fearful and what precautions they had adopted
in light of the "high" incidence of violent crime against women in
Toronto, structured and confined the answers to certain limits. Without
observational evidence, we are unable to ascertain whether this
occurred. However, observational research literature in general would
suggest it is highly likely that this was the practice (e.g. Tuchman,
1978, Fishman, 1978), and we were told by a reporter that this was a
regular practice in the newspaper he worked for during the attacks on
women moral panic. Furthermore, it is noteworthy that there were no
published statements from women suggesting that they were not taking
precautions. The only differing opinion offered was of the type cited
in the feature article reproduced in the last chapter (p. 54): of 25
women interviewed, 22 expressed fear and were said to be taking
precautions, and the remaining 3 said they were not fearful but would
have been if they had not shut off radio news and refused to read
newspaper items regarding attacks on women.

Another possible explanation is that women, lacking any other source of information concerning rape, simply accept and repeat what they hear and read in the media. Graber (1980), reports that 95% of citizens she interviewed said the news media were their primary source of information about crime and criminal justice. Individual women may follow the "common sense" of authorized knowers and repeat it for the use of the news media.

Another possibility is that women may focus on the actions of victims as the locus of the problem because by doing so it is comforting to them. If attacks on women are understood to occur to those women who behave inappropriately, who have not taken the proper precautions, then other women have a simple way of protecting themselves, adopting those precautions. Thus, it can be argued that women accept certain images of attacks on women and the implications for the restriction of their own behaviour that go along with this because it is comforting to feel that one has self-control over a particular situation.

Young (1981) offers some theorizing which may bear on this explanation. He emphasizes the need to situate news media consensual ideology in the material reality which gives rise to it. Young discusses two contrasting spheres in societal structure: the world as it appears from the level of the process of circulation and the world from the level of the process of produciton. In the sphere of circulation there is the idea of the worker selling labour freely and receiving a fair exchange for it. In the sphere of production we find instead of freedom, coercion and necessity; instead of formal equality, substantive inequality; instead of equivalence, exploitation. "...The phenomenal form (freedom, equality, equivalence) inverts and obfuscates reality (servitude, inequality, exploitation) but it is not a mere illusion" (ibid: 245). It is not that one sphere is any more real than the other, rather reality is constituted by both spheres.

> Thus, the images used by the mass media
> tied as they are to the world of

> appearances, are not mere illusions. It is
> their cognitive fit with reality that
> explains their credibility, it is their
> real sense of justice that generates
> support for them among the people rather
> than mere bad faith and mystification.
> (ibid: 246)

Women may accept this dominant image of rape and the implications that it has for their own social control because having adopted these day to day measures in their lives they have not experienced such an attack. Thus, the dominant image fits their day to day reality.

Another view of the implications of our findings for the social control of women is provided by considering the research literature on rape.

There are many 'common sense' conceptions of rape, concerning the type of women who become rape victims, the type of men who rape, the relationship between the victim and the offender, the circumstances surrounding the offence, and the reasons or motivations for such acts.

One image of rape is that it is a 'street crime', one that occurs in dark alleys, secluded parks and underground parking garages. Indeed, as we have seen, authorized knowers often advise women to stay out of public places late at night as one of the precautionary measures which they can adopt to avoid being a victim of rape. However, researchers who have examined this phenomenon have found that rape is just as likely to occur in the private realm. Menachem Amir (1971) in his study of 646 rapes known to the police in Philadelphia, discovered that 56% of these rapes took place in either the home of the participant, or a friend or relative. Clark and Lewis (1977), in their study of rapes reported to the Metropolitan Toronto police force, found that 53% of these rapes occurred in some type of private residence, while 47% occurred in either a public place or a vehicle. It appears that, "...the domestic realm contains as many dangers of rape for women as do more public and impersonal places..." (Smart and Smart, 1978:92).

An important question which must be addressed is the origin of these images. As previously emphasized, researchers have argued that in today's increasingly segregated society, people have little if any first hand experience with many phenomena, including crime, or more specifically in the context of this discussion, rape (see Wilkins, 1973; Hall et al., 1978; Heath, Gordon & LeBailly, 1980; Gordon & Heath, 1981; Graber, 1980). Their perceptions are thus formed on the basis of indirect information and images, such as the experiences of friends, or the consumption of cultural products such as television serials, films, news, novels, and plays.

The image can serve ideologically, as a means not to know, in a manner which has implications for social control. As Griffen (1971:331) states,

> The threat of rape is used to deny women
> employment...The fear of rape keeps women
> off the streets at night. Keeps women at
> home. Keeps women passive and modest for
> fear that they be thought provocative.

Smart and Smart (1978) have argued that it is not so much the fear of rape itself that acts as a form of social control over women, but rather it is the internalisation by women, via the process of socialization, of the possibility of rape. They conducted a study which examined the content of rape reports in newspapers, focusing on the presentation of the victim, the descriptions of the offender, the explanations of the incident, and any attributions of motive and responsibility for the assault. The results of their analysis support the argument that newspapers, while not necessarily creating widely held misperceptions of rape, were by the content and style of their reports likely to strengthen them. Smart and Smart found that when accounts of motivation were represented in the newspapers they tended to perpetuate the commonly held belief that rape is simply the outcome of sexual frustration or arousal. They also found, as was found in our research, that in many instances the news report contained a warning or a caution to women, such as where not to walk, what time not to go out, how not to behave, and what not to wear.   They concluded that,

> ...the general form and content
> of rape reporting serve to
> confound a rational
> understanding of rape as well as
> to indirectly conspire to
> perpetuate women's social and
> sexual subordination by
> producing rape reports which
> serve as both sexual titillation
> as a veiled 'warning' to non-
> conforming'independent' women,
> that is to say as an implicit
> form of social control. (ibid,
> 1978: 91).

Erikson, following Durkheim, has argued that

> an enormous amount of modern
> 'news' is devoted to reports
> about deviant behaviour and its
> punishment: indeed the largest
> circulation newspaper in the
> United States prints very little
> else. Yet how do we explain
> what makes these items
> 'newsworthy' or why they command
> the great attention they do?
> Perhaps they satisfy a number of
> psychological perversities among
> the mass audience, as
> commentators sometimes point
> out, but at the same time they
> constitute our main source of
> information about normative
> contours of society. In a
> figurative sense, at least,
> morality and immorality meet at
> the public scaffold, and it is
> during this meeting that the
> community declares where the
> line between them should be
> drawn. (Erikson, 1962: 28)

It can be argued that the content of attacks on women reports in the newspapers that concentrate on the actions of the victim just prior to the attack, contain within them implicit warnings to women of the possible consequences of overstepping the acceptable, "common sense" behaviours. These implicit warnings are made explicit by journalists in the opinion columns and editorials, experts and organizational representatives in news stories and news features, and by individual citizens in the news features and in the letters they write. Thus, the police and the experts are mobilized to advise women on the acceptable, "common sense" behaviours they must adopt to avoid attack. The news stories of the occurrences, via their concentration on the victim's actions immediately prior to the attack, demonstrate the possible consequences of overstepping these boundaries, while at the same time further demarcating these boundaries.

Underlying this dominant image is a traditional concept of male and female sexuality, which assumes that males are naturally aggressive and females are naturally submissive. This view conceptualizes rape to be a natural act which arises in situations where men, unrestrained by convention or the threat of punishment, will rape. The major way to put a stop to rape is to prevent dangerous situations from occurring at all, and secondarily by providing a law enforcement and punishment system to control dangerous aggressors. These two solutions were quite frequently endorsed in the three newspapers.

Anthropological studies have demonstrated that sexual attitudes and practices are learned and not instinctual, and in many societies rape is unknown. In our contemporary society men and women are trained to believe that the sexual act involves domination. Normal heterosexual relationships are conceptualized as an aggressive male forcing himself on a submissive female. In such a society there is a very close relationship between violence and sexuality (cf. Herman, 1977).

A recent analysis suggests that this dominant perception of rape and the laws dealing with rape are grounded in a deep rooted conception of rape as a property violation. Where sex is viewed as commodity, 'respectable' women are those who are or will be at some future point the exclusive sexual property of one man. From this view rape is the theft of one man's sexual property by another (Clark and Lewis, 1977:116, see also the concluding discussion of this chapter at pp. 91-94). This system of thought further requires that women take necessaryprecautions to protect that which makes them valuable. The dominant perception of rape in this society, the everyday social reactions, as well as the reactions of the legal system, have incorporated the implicit theme that there are, in effect, particular social circumstances under which men are somehow excused from attacking women.

Brownmiller (1975:449) argues that the continuous fear of rape, the need to protect against it, and to adopt certain behaviour patterns that will not be deemed to encourage it, impairs women's autonomy:

> The ultimate effect of rape upon the woman's mental and emotional health is accomplished even without the act. For to accept a special burden of self protection is to reinforce the concept that women must live and move about in fear and can never expect to achieve the personal freedom, independence, and self-assurance of men.

It can be argued that the dominant image of rape which appeared in the three newspapers may contribute to this effect.

The tendency to be suspicious of rape claims and to impute impropriety to the victim is pervasive. Women are often implicitly blamed for the offence. This tendency may be encouraged by the frequently voiced thesis of 'victim precipitation'.

> The concept of victim precipitation (VP) rests on another model: victim-doer-victim. Here, the victim is the one who is acting out, initiating the interaction between her and the offender, and by her behaviour she generates the potentiality for criminal behaviour of the offender or triggers this potentiality, if it existed before in him. (Amir, 1971:259).

The problem with such theorizing is that

> as a post facto conclusion ... a finding of
> victim precipitation depends upon the
> perspective of the largely male police,
> prosecutors, and judges who appraise the
> case. The concept of victim precipitation
> hinges primarily on the male definitions of
> expressed or implied consent to engage in
> sexual relations, and is shaped by
> traditional restrictive stereotypes of
> women (Chappell, Geis and Geis, 1977:72).

As Schur (1980) has argued, it is one thing to suggest that if a given woman had not been out alone late at night she would not, in that circumstance, have been raped, but it is quite another to suggest that women should not be free to be out alone late at night and that by doing so they actively precipitate their assault. "...Failure to meet unwarranted burdens of self protective behaviour should not become a basis for impugning a person's basic character or for considering their reports untrustworthy" (Schur, 1980: 165; see also Schur, 1984).

It can be concluded that

> in so far as a press report of rape never
> seeks to explain or address the existence
> of the general phenomenon of rape but
> merely selectively focuses on a specific
> instance, the account which is provided is
> structured in terms of the surface details
> of the specific case concerned. As a
> result the underlying structuring of social
> and sexual relations, which both produce
> the possibility of rape and make specific
> social locations and circumstances likely
> venues for rape, remain undisclosed in
> press accounts. Thereby the conventional
> wisdoms concerning rape are upheld, namely
> that women who get raped are in some sense
> responsible for their own fate, could in
> fact have avoided their suffering by not
> putting themseles at risk by entering the
> specific social space or territory within
> which the rape occurred (Smart and Smart,
> 1978:101).

Heath, Gordon and LeBailly (1980) examined the portrayal of rape in eight different newspapers from three American cities. They compared the 'facts' of rape from victimization studies to the 'facts' from the representation of rape in the newspapers. The overall picture of rape in the newspapers had a surprising degree of agreement with the overall picture that was provided from victimization studies. However, the interesting finding in relation to the question we have posed is that the areas of disagreement tended to arise from the newspapers' almost exclusive reliance on the police for their information. These researchers felt that the distortion of rape incidents in press accounts is related to the type of rape situations that are not reported to the police and to the practice by the police of systematically classifying as 'unfounded' certain kinds of rape situations. For example, 50% of all rapes reported in a United States Law Enforcement Assistance Administration victimization survey were reported to have occurred between 6 p.m. and midnight. However, only 5% of all rapes reported in the newspapers occurred during this time period. The researchers argue that rapes in the course of a date are more likely to occur during this time period. These are furthermore the type of rape situations that have the highest probability of going unreported, or if reported, have the highest probability of being classified as unfounded by the police.

Drawing from our discussion of the traditional concepts of male and female sexuality, this tendency to not report rapes that have occurred in such circumstances, and the tendency on the part of the police to classify them as unfounded, can be understood. This traditional conception requires women to adopt certain precautionary measures to protect that which makes them valuable. Being attacked while on a date suggests that the woman did not choose carefully enough who to go out with, and thus placed her sexual property, which she has the obligation to protect, in jeopardy.

Women who are raped in these situations may learn of likely difficulties in having the case processed by the police and the courts should they report the rape, and thus may be inclined not to report. The police, on the other hand, do not necessarily classify these types of rape situations as 'unfounded' because they do not believe that the rape has taken place. Rather, they are aware that such rapes will make very poor cases in court. The chances that the offender, if apprehended, will be convicted are very slim. The police, operating under various organizational constraints, are concerned with likely success of prosecution, and may be as a consequence more inclined to classify a rape case as "founded" if they know or are reasonably assured that it will result in a conviction. In terms of news reports, rapes classified as "unfounded" by the police will not normally be passed on to the media. Therefore the public, who obtain most of their information concerning rape from the news media, are rarely made aware of the other social circumstances in which rape may take place.

Certainly the attacks on women moral panic we studied was portrayed as a problem of _public_ safety. Formulations about the nature of the problem and remedies thus emphasized restriction on the use of public places: primarily "educating" women to restrict themselves, but also improving police surveillance and patrol, and doing something about "dangerous" men who may be likely to attack. Again our point is not that this is somehow unreasonable discourse, but it is limited and in that sense ideological. Moreover, its effect is to rule out, usually by exclusion, other discourses which might lead to a different understanding and knowledge. Another possible effect is that it reinforced the view of women that they should be their own social control agents in their property relations with men.

Conclusion

This is a modest and limited study of the nature of news as it pertains to the communication of public problems. It focuses upon one theme in the news, at one point in time, in one location. The data are also limited by the interpretive categorizations imposed, and by the

fact that data collection was mainly restricted to content analysis.
Chibnall (1977), Tuchman (1978), and Fishman (1980), among many others,
have observed routine practices of news production to elucidate how
newsworkers' organizational constraints and working ideologies reproduce
dominant cultural images; observational data would have expanded our
understanding of the attacks on women theme as it was constituted in the
three newspapers. Although limited in these ways, our findings are
consistent with other research on particular moral panics, provide more
systematic data on some aspects than have previous researchers, and
offer some additional knowledge.

The manufacturing of moral panics appears to provide for the range
of general functions served by the news media. It is intended to draw a
readership interested in being entertained and titillated as the socio-
drama unfolds, thereby engaging people in a manner similar to other
forms of popular drama. In the process it provides for a steady supply
of material that meets organizational demands for copy and for items
which "sell" the newspaper to the readership. It provides a vehicle by
which the news media can perform a "fourth estate" function, questioning
various public authorities about what actions they are going to take,
forcing them to be accountable.

On an ongoing basis, the reporting of a moral panic provides the
cultural function of giving signs of the moral contours of society. As
Erikson (1962, 1966) in particular has taught us, following Durkheim,
the moral boundaries of societies are very elastic indeed. In turn,
there is considerable relativity in the conceptions of problems and in
recommendations for their solutions. This can be readily appreciated by
contrasting the news accounts of attacks on women we have studied,
including the sources cited, locus of the problem, and proposed
solutions, with a contemporary debate concerning rape and property
values in Zimbabwe.

PARLIAMENT

"MP's unite in call for harsh rape penalties"

Several members of Parliament yesterday urged the Government to impose tougher penalties for cases of rape, with some suggesting hanging, life imprisonment and others 30 to 50 year jail terms.

The MPs -- from Zanu (PF), the Independents and the Republican Front - were responding to a motion introduced by the Zapu member for Matabeleland North, Mrs. Ruth Chinamano.

Her motion calls on the Assembly to "abhor the general decline in respect of law and order, particularly the upsurge in crimes of rape of women and young girls, and considers that the sentences imposed for such crimes are too lenient".

Cde Chinamano said rape was a "plague" that was demeaning the women of Zimbabwe. She cited 24 reported cases of rape published in The Herald, in which some of the victims were eight-year-old children.

'DISEASE'

"This disease has spread throughout the whole country," she said. "I do not know what kind of a nation we are bringing up. These children will spit on our graves if we do not find a solution to this deplorable epidemic."

She was supported by fellow Zapu member for Matabeleland South, Cde Peter Njini, who proposed that sentences be raised to 30 or 50 years imprisonment for convicted rapists.

The former Deputy Minister of Community Development and Women's Affairs, Bishop-Joshua Dhube, said rape interfered with the girl's "bargaining power" in the form of "chastity and virginity", and prejudiced her chances of getting a good husband.

> As a deterrent, Bishop Dhube suggested, the
> convicted rapist, must marry the girl.
>
> "The boy who does not want to marry the
> girl must be shut up in prison to die there
> so that he will have no chance to spoil
> another girl."
>
> A married man convicted of rape or a man
> who raped another person's wife "must be
> hanged", he said. (The Herald, Zimbabwe,
> February 3, 1984).

Compared to what we have studied, this article indicates relativity. There is a different set of preferred solutions, as well as a somewhat more explicit conception of women-as-property. What is the same is that it is the newspaper which communicates who are the authorized knowers, what they claim is a problem, and what they propose as solutions. Perhaps more signifcant than anything else it does, the newspaper provides a daily "reading" of public culture, a perpetual barometer of public problems and their solutions, making evident prevailing images of the shifting moral boundaries of society.

While the manufacturing of a moral panic serves these functions and provides images, it does not offer very much in the way of knowledge. Understanding in terms of social process and social structure is not evident. Indeed, in the very process of not providing for such knowledge, newspapers essentially reproduce the consensual ideology of the dominant culture. Ironically the newspapers' sustained barrage of fear and loathing over disorder does not provide knowledge, it simply acknowledges order.

BIBLIOGRAPHY

Amir, M.
  1971   _Patterns in Forcible Rape._ Chicago: University of
          Chicago Press.

Becker, H.
  1967   "Whose Side are We On?" _Social Problems_ 14: 239-247.

Berger, P. and T. Luckmann
  1967   _The Social Construction of Reality._ New York: Doubleday.

Brownmiller, S.
  1975   _Against Our Will: Men, Women and Rape._ New York: Bantam
          Books.

Chappel, D., R. Geis and G. Geis (eds.)
  1977   _Forcible Rape: The Crime, the Victim, and the Offender._ New
          York: Columbia University Press.

Chibnall, S.
  1977   _Law and Order News: An Analysis of Crime Reporting in the
          British Press._ London: Tavistock.

Clark, L. and D. Lewis
  1977   _Rape: The Price of Coercive Sexuality._ Toronto: The
          Women's Press.

Cohen, S.
  1972   _Folk Devils and Moral Panics._ London: MacGibbon and Kee.

Cohen, S. and J. Young (eds.)
  1973   _The Manufacture of News: Social Problems, Deviance and the
          Mass Media._ London: Constable.

Ditton, J. and J. Duffy
  1982   _Bias in Newspaper Crime Reports: Selected and Distorted
          Reporting of Crime News in 6 Scottish Newspapers During
          March, 1981._ Background Paper Number 3, Department of
          Sociology, University of Glasgow.

Dussuyer, I.
  1979   _Crime News: A Study of 40 Ontario Newspapers._ Toronto:
          Centre of Criminology, University of Toronto.

Epstein, E.
  1974   _News from Nowhere._ New York: Vintage.

Ericson, R.
  1981   _Making Crime._ Toronto: Butterworths.

Ericson, R.
  1982   Reproducing Order. Toronto: University of Toronto Press.

Erikson, K.T.
  1962   "Notes on the Sociology of Deviance," Social Problems 9:
          307-314.

Erikson, K.T.
  1966   Wayward Puritans: A Study in the Sociology of Deviance. New
          York: John Wiley.

Fishman, M.
  1978   "Crime Waves as Ideology," Social Problems 25: 531-543.

Fishman, M.
  1980   Manufacturing the News. Austin: University of Texas Press.

Garofalo, J.
  1981   "Crime and the Mass Media: A Selective Review of Research,"
          Journal of Research in Crime and Delinquency 18: 319-350.

Goffman, E.
  1974   Frame Analysis: An Essay on the Organization of Experience.
          Cambridge, Mass.: Harvard University Press.

Gordon, M. and L. Heath
  1981   "The News Business, Crime and Fear," in D. Lewis (ed.)
          Reactions to Crime. Beverly Hills: Sage.

Graber, D.
  1980   Crime News and the Public. New York: Praeger.

Griffen, S.
  1977   "Rape: The All-American Crime," in D. Chappel et al. (eds.)
          Forcible Rape: The Crime, the Victim and the Offender. New
          York: Columbia University Press.

Gusfield, J.
  1981   The Culture of Public Problems. Chicago: University of
          Chicago Press.

Hall, S.
  1979   "Culture, the Media and the 'Ideological Effect'," in J.
          Curran et al. (eds.) Mass Communication and Society. Beverly
          Hills: Sage.

Hall, S. et al.
  1978   Policing the Crisis. London: MacMillan.

Hartley, J.
  1982   Understanding News. London: Methuen.

Heath, L., M. Gordon, and R. LeBailly
    1980   "What Newspapers Tell Us (and Don't Tell Us) about Rape," in
             press.

Herman, D.
    1979   "The Rape Culture," in J. Freeman (ed.) Women: A Feminist
             Perspective (2nd edition) Palo Alto, Cal.: Mayfield
             Publishing.

Kelling, G.
    1983   "On the Accomplishments of the Police," in M. Punch (ed.)
             Control in the Police Organization. Cambridge, Mass.:
             M.I.T. Press.

Ng, Y.
    1981   "Ideology, Media, and Moral Panics: An Analysis of the
             Jacques Murder," M.A. dissertation, Centre of Criminology,
             University of Toronto.

Punch, M. (ed.)
    1983   Control in the Police Organization. Cambridge, Mass.:
             M.I.T. Press.

Robertson, S.M.
    1981   Courts and the Media. Toronto: Butterworths.

Rock, P.
    1973   "News as Eternal Recurrence," in S. Cohen and J. Young, The
             Manufacture of News. Beverly Hills: Sage.

Rothman, D.
    1980   Conscience and Convenience. Boston: Little Brown.

Royal Commission on Newspapers
    1981   Final Report. Ottawa: Information Canada.

Royal Commission on Newspapers
    1981a   The Journalists. Ottawa: Research Studies on the Newspaper
             Industry, Volume 2.

Royal Commission on Newspapers
    1981b   The Newspaper and Public Affairs. Ottawa: Research Studies
             on the Newspaper Industry, Volume 7.

Royal Commission on Newspapers

    1981c   Labour Relations in the Newspaper Industry. Ottawa:
             Research Studies on the Newspaper Industry, Volume 5.

Ryan, W.
    1971   Blaming the Victim. New York: Vintage Books.

Sacks, H.
1972   "On the Analyzability of Stories by Children," in J. Gumperz
            and D. Hymes (eds.) Directions in Sociolinguistics.   New
            York: Holt, Rinehart and Winston.

Schur, E.
1980   The Politics of Deviance: Stigma Contests and Uses of Power.
            Englewood Cliffs, N.J.:   Prentice-Hall.

Schur, E.
1984   Labeling Women Deviant: Gender, Stigma, and Social Control.
            New York: Random House.

Smart, C. and B. Smart
1978   "Accounting for Rape: Reality and Myth in Press Reporting,"
            in C. Smart and B. Smart (eds.) Women, Sexuality and Social
            Control. London: Routledge and Kegan Paul.

Taylor, I.
1980   "The Law and Order Issue in the British General Election and
            Canadian Federal Election of 1979: Crime, Populism and the
            State," Canadian Journal of Sociology 5: 285-311.

Tuchman, G.
1978   Making News: A Study in the Construction of Reality. New
            York: Free Press.

Wilkins, L.
1973   "Information and the Definition of Deviance," in S. Cohen and
            J. Young (eds.) The Manufacture of News: Social Problems,
            Deviance, and the Mass Media. London: Constable.

Young, J.
1981   "The Manufacture of News: A Critique of the Present
            Convergence in Mass Media Theory," in State Control of
            Information in the Field of Deviance and Social Control.
            European Group for the Study of Deviance and Social Control,
            Working Papers in European Criminology, No. 2.